Paula's Window

Papa, the Bielski Partisans and A Life Unexpected

Liberation, painted by Paula Burger, 2003

By Paula Burger

As Told to Andrea Jacobs

Paula's Window:
Papa, the Bielski Partisans and A Life Unexpected

ISBN: 978-1-938859-47-2

Library of Congress

Paula Burger
P.O. Box 221532
Denver, Colorado 80222
burgerart@gmail.com

Andrea Jacobs
ajljacobs@comcast.net

Dedication

To my parents Sarah and Wolf Koladicki. They hold my most beautiful and painful memories.

To my brother Isaac, with whom I spent three frightening years of my childhood.

And to my children and grandchildren. You are the light that vanquishes the darkness.

Acknowledgements

I want to thank Robert Bielski for his friendship and guidance, but most of all for keeping the memory of Tuvia Bielski alive. More than anyone, he has ensured his father's place of honor in history, and in our hearts.

I need to single out my children Susan, Freda, Steve and Robbyn. Raised under the shadow of my story, they read the drafts of this book with fresh eyes and unique insight. This narrative flows in their blood, yet they never tire of hearing it. When I speak to students about the Holocaust, my children often accompany me. They hold me up time and again.

Many people helped nurture this book along the way, particularly my daughter Freda and granddaughter Jessica for contributing their excellent editing skills, Rabbi Selwyn Franklin, Audrey Friedman Marcus, Phyllis and Arnold Hayutin, Jon Tandler and graphic artist Seiji Nagata. Their assistance is deeply appreciated.

My brother Isaac Koll, who was at my side in the Holocaust, gave me free reign to tell our story. All he ever asked was, "How is the book coming?" My sister Fay was also unfailingly supportive.

For two-and-a-half years, as I shared my experiences at this kitchen table every Sunday, my husband Sam busied himself in another room. I never asked him to do this. He instinctively understood my need for privacy.

Sam, you are the love of my life.

Finally, I must thank Andrea Jacobs. She possesses a rare and beautiful gift — a heart that hears. Without her talent, dedication, sensitivity and compassion, this book would not exist.

Paula Burger,

Denver, Colorado

Foreword

In July of 1944, the order from Russia arrived. The Nazis had been driven back, the Bielski *Otriad* (partisan detachment) was instructed to disband, and all the survivors — Jews who hid in the Naliboki forest for years — were supposed to return to Novogrudek, Poland. The partisans were told to destroy all remnants of the camp to prevent retreating German soldiers hiding in the woods from setting up a base.

And so early in the morning, the partisans broke windows, wrecked their huts, and buried their tools and utensils. They blew up the whole camp and assembled for departure, lining up two by two in a straight line. That line extended over two kilometers.

They marched in military order, with the armed units leading the way. They entered Novogrudek and saw the extent of the damage. The Jewish community was no more. More than 1,250 Bielski Jews dispersed to the corners of the world.

Those 1,250 brave souls rebuilt their families through the ensuing decades. Today, more than 20,000 Jewish people who were not supposed to be here proudly proclaim that they do exist.

As the son of Tuvia Bielski, the legendary commander of the Bielski partisans, I always see my father's reflection radiating from the word, "hero." However, as I've grown older, I look at the word hero from several angles. The natural inclination is to associate my father with hero in one breath, but now I also look at the survivors and their descendants almost the same way.

We all know that millions of Holocaust victims had no choice. They faced the barrel of a gun pointed at their heads. They were led to their slaughter like sheep. We can never minimize the suffering, or the utter lack of choice when one's life is left in the hands of the enemy.

Our story is different. Our ancestors who were part of the Bielski *Otriad* had a choice — either wait out the Nazi invasion and hope the situation improves, or escape to the forests and an uncertain tomorrow. Yet the trees and dense shrubbery of that forest, along with the pragmatic leader Tuvia Bielski looming ten feet tall on his horse, provided hope, courage, resistance and heroism to the inhabitants of the group.

As the years pass and the original partisans dwindle, it is their legacy and the growth of their descendants that inspire all of us to continue to grow as families and as a people.

Although we are not blood related, there is this familial kinship that resounds between the descendants. We are a family. We are all closely related — not by choice, but by the overwhelming hardships endured by our parents during this darkest of times.

When I speak of my father's accomplishments throughout the world, I have met many people who come up to me and say, "Your father saved my life." Although that has occurred many times in many places, I never tire of hearing it and still get emotional when someone attributes his or her survival to my father.

In 2004, I spoke at the child survivors' conference in Denver, Colorado. After my speech, this short, spry, meticulously dressed woman approached me and introduced herself. Her name was Paula Burger.

She began with the words, "Your father saved my life and the lives of my father and younger brother."

As I gazed into this woman's eyes, emotions quickly got

the better of me. I realized that there was something special about this woman. Paula and I instantly bonded with each other.

Although I went through the majority of my life not knowing her, it felt as if I had known Paula all of my life. In fact, I *have* known Paula all my life. Being born into this amazing story of survival has established this unbreakable bond with all the survivors and their families.

Paula's story brings the pain and suffering of her experience to the forefront so that her family, students and all generations to come will learn of the evil brutality that Paula, her brother Isaac and her father Wolf endured.

They are the heroes, because they are the survivors.

Robert Bielski

New York, NY

When Snow was Sweet

A child can get lost watching the snow — the way it weaves and chases itself before collapsing to the ground. I was a child once, near Novogrudek, Poland. I'd stare for hours out the window as snowflakes fell like feathers on the grass. This was before the war, when snow was still sweet.

On Shabbos (the Jewish Sabbath), my father Wolf Koladicki would set me up high on his shoulders and carry me through the snow to the wooden *shul*. It was warm inside, and people prayed in a strange language. I wrapped myself inside a thick velvet curtain hiding from the rhythmic din until it was time to leave.

It was a long walk back to our ranch outside Novogrudek. My father distracted me with stories that always contained a subtle moral. I never responded well to black-and-white orders: "This is right, this is wrong." But you remember a story forever.

After a while, he let me slide from his arms and held my hand all the way home. Our footprints sang in the whiteness. The journey culminated in the arms of my mother Sarah, who would pick me up and spin me around the shiny floor.

Papa was born in Yatra, not far from Novogrudek. An enterprising young man with pale skin, dark hair and street smarts, he possessed a remarkable head for business. People gravitated toward him, trusted him. He was such an exceptional man — intuitive, successful, and absolutely fearless. The expression "I can't do that" had no place in his vocabulary. He did whatever was necessary to protect his family.

I remember the games we played. He would position me on top of a large wardrobe, spread out his hands and say, "Jump!" From my three-year-old vantage point, he stood miles away. But my timidity merely intensified the joy.

In another "secret game," my father would hold out candy and ask me, "Who do you love more, me or your mother?" I was torn. I was addicted to candy. But I understood that anything I said would be wrong. So I closed my eyes, and my mouth. Papa laughed and gave me the candy anyway. My parents nourished me with unconditional love, which has made all the difference in my life.

Even as I talk about her, I can't see Mama's face. I have no photographs to unlock the memories. My father always spoke

of my mother with devoted, almost painful admiration —
her beauty, her intelligence, her refinement.

Before they met, Mama studied pharmacy at the University of Vilna, where enforced quotas restricted the number of
Jewish students. Mama had to stand in the back of the classroom but refused to bend to the anti-Semitism that robbed
other young women of their aspirations. She received her
degree and practiced pharmacy in Novogrudek until she met
my father, whose dreams equaled hers.

Sarah Ginienski — they called her Sorka — had three
brothers, Shepa, Meyer and Joseph, and three older sisters,
Rivka, Chana and Grunya. Back then, it was customary to
find husbands for the eldest daughters first.

My grandparents arranged for a *shadchen*, or matchmaker,
to gather a list of potential spouses. When young men came
to the house to share a meal with one of the eligible sisters,
my grandparents hid my mother in the attic.

One day, as my father was leaving my family's house, my
mother looked down from the attic window. He glanced up
at the same moment. This accidental encounter sealed their
fate, and mine.

The next time Papa visited the house, he asked my grandparents, "Where is the girl I saw in the attic?" "She's not here," they insisted. So he kept returning, week after week. Finally they were introduced. I like to compare their love to a romance novel. Tragically, fate parted them much too soon.

My father and mother worked together in their grocery store and restaurant in Perisheke, a suburb of Novogrudek. In addition to other business concerns, my father constantly bought land.

Their first child died of a heart defect. When I was born in 1934, my parents transferred all their love and hope to me. I was doubly blessed. I knew what it was like to be the apple of someone's eye.

I slept in my grandmother Feige Ginienski's room, but not out of necessity. Our house was spacious by anyone's standards. Acres of land caressed its edges. I was pampered. I had a nanny. My mother employed Polish peasants to help in the home.

Yet I always felt that the peasants feigned their affection. There was nothing genuine or reciprocal in our relationship. They were nice to us because we provided their livelihood.

We were Jewish; they were Polish. Anti-Semitism, like the bitter winters, was a predictable season.

Novogrudek's Jewish community, one of the oldest in Lithuania, first appears in a 1529 historical document. Whether it belonged to Latvia or Russia or Belarus, Novo-grudek remained a relatively stable environment for Jews. At the time of my birth, 6,000 Jews lived in Novogrudek and comprised half the population. In the intervening centuries, the region went through numerous political hands and iden-tities.

Near the end of the 19th century, eminent rabbis had founded renowned yeshivas (institutions of higher learning) that transformed the town into a major center of Jewish learning, life and observance. Almost every emerging Jewish movement was represented. By the early 1930s, Zionism, *musar* (an ethical, educational and cultural philosophy), Hebrew and Yiddish schools, a religious day school, two Yiddish weeklies, soup kitchens and a Yiddish theater flour-ished in Novogrudek.

I was six and too young for school, but observation makes a wonderful textbook. During the spring and summer, Mama tended cucumbers, lettuce, tomatoes and radishes in our large garden. When hard berries dropped to the ground from trees and bushes, I collected them and sewed them together with a needle and thread. My poor grandmother would cry, "You're letting the girl hold a needle? *Oy, oy!*"

Isaac was born in 1939. He was the most adorable child. I wasn't at all jealous when they brought him home from the hospital and laid him on a white lace blanket that covered his tiny body. Actually I was relieved, because I no longer occupied center stage. I had more time to explore my universe: the rolling hills of the countryside, the multicolored wildflowers, my image in the mirror and my eager imagination.

One of my aunts owned an ice cream parlor in town and she always gave me ice cream when we stopped in the store. Once I wandered outside and looked down the street. There was a big hill, and I couldn't see beyond it. To me, it was the end of the world. I had to find out what was on the other side. But after walking and walking, I discovered it was just a hill, not the gateway to an exciting adventure.

Suddenly I panicked. I was lost, separated from my parents and all things familiar. The ice cream cone that had emboldened my behavior was gone. Finally Mama found me. It's comforting to recall a time when being lost was so easily remedied.

Memories die a protracted death. The decades gradually devour names, places and dates. Faces melt like ice cream on a hot day. But sometimes an image emerges with unexplained, undeniable clarity.

I remember a Friday evening in our home. It's Shabbos. I am six, maybe a little older. Papa isn't there. He has been consigned to mandatory work detail with the other male Jews. The Nazis care nothing for the setting sun. Papa rarely makes it home before Shabbos.

Isaac sleeps in his crib. My mother lights the candles. Although her expression is barely perceptible, I can almost touch Mama's face in the candles' glow. I feel the tension hanging in the room. All the Jews are on edge, including my mother.

After reciting the blessing over the candles, Mama sits next to my chair and cradles me in her arms. I am inside a cocoon — safe, protected and loved. All through the war, as our situation deteriorated, I returned to that image again and again.

The Sky Exploded

For seven years my world was confined to lovely daydreams and the soft thrill of the morning, when everything was so inviting. World War II actually began for us in 1939, when the Red Army crossed the Russian-Polish border as part of the Molotov-Ribbentrop Agreement. Western Belarus was annexed, and Novogrudek became the district capital of Grodno.

At least a thousand Jews fled the Nazis who were storming into eastern and western Poland. Some found sanctuary on my parents' land. Late at night, when their own children were asleep, these nomadic Jews told my parents unbearable stories of the Nazis' savagery.

The Russians had their own brand of anti-Semitism, but they treated us fairly well. I used to watch the soldiers browse in our shops. They loved the nightgowns, which they mistook for dresses and proudly sent home to their wives. Despite the bad news and images that no doubt kept them up at night, my parents tried to maintain a semblance of normalcy. They wanted to hear my laughter another month, another week, another day.

By 1940, rumors and whispers became permanent guests in our home. My parents waited until my brother and I left the room before unburdening their minds to each other. But I never wandered too far away. I closed the door but listened long and hard to their words.

Then, on a summer day in 1941, the sky exploded and our lives came tumbling down. I saw flashes on the horizon, leaving behind smoky red plumes larger than monster tails. Planes flew so close that bullets scraped the ground right where I played. My parents yanked me inside, rebuking me while they cried and held me close.

The Russians scattered in defeat, and many Jews ran with them to Minsk or Lida. The majority, like my family, remained. Beatings and killings became commonplace. My playmates vanished. Some of my cousins disappeared. I don't know what happened to them. The dead don't share their secrets. From then on, my parents never let Isaac or me out of their sight.

The Nazis invaded Novogrudek on July 3-4, 1941. Anti-Jewish laws took effect immediately. Jews lost all citizenship rights. Jews handed over their valuables to the authorities. Jews could not walk on the sidewalks or streets. The Star of David we had to sew on our outer garments took the guess-work out of hate. Now we were easier to spot, and impossible to ignore. Soon I wore the yellow star on my navy blue coat like a badge. I was not allowed outside without it.

I hid with my family on the ranch, but none of us could hide from the truth anymore. I did not exist. Death squads — the *Sicherheitsdienst*, the Orpo, Gestapo, Waffen SS, the criminal police — conducted roundups with eager abandon. On Shabbos, July 26, 1941, Jewish doctors and professionals were ordered to stand in rows of five in the marketplace. The Nazis killed 52 men. I was not there to witness their agony.

I had sensed fear before in the seconds before jumping into my father's arms from the wardrobe. Now I felt its furious fists beat inside my chest. Perhaps Papa heard the pounding through our hugs. He started making plans.

My father had a large network of friends and business acquaintances. I'm fairly certain he met Tuvia and Zus Bielski, the two older Bielski brothers, before the war. They had family in Novogrudek and traveled to our town on business. Somehow Papa learned about the massacres and roundups. If he had to be away, he got word to my mother and told her where to take us, and who was willing to hide us.

One frigid December night, the Nazis crept into our remote area to round up Jews. My father wasn't home. "Wake up," my mother urged. "Get dressed. We are leaving now." It was very late. She picked up Isaac, took my hand and pushed us outside into the howling snow. We walked and walked. Ice pellets hit my face and snowdrifts swallowed my legs.

I kept crying, "Mama, I'm too tired, I can't walk anymore." And my mother said, "Papa will be there, Papa will be there." So I continued walking. We finally stopped at a small hut. Polish peasants clutching their robes ushered us inside. They weren't happy.

After a couple of days, we returned to the ranch. I found out later that thousands of Jews died in the first mass execution in Novogrudek — maybe the very night Mama brought us through the snow to safety. Survivors refer to the massacre as "Black Monday."

It began on Friday, December 5, 1941. Nazi officials, soldiers, Polish police and members of the *Judenrat*, the Nazi-controlled Jewish council, went door to door ordering all Jewish men, women and children to report to the courthouse. Snow fell heavily, and the temperatures slipped below zero. Two days later, the men were forced to dismantle a fence and carry it to Pereshika, where my father had a store.

On Monday, December 8, the Jews were ordered to stand in lines. Skilled laborers went to the right. The majority — women, children, the elderly and the sick — went to the left, where trucks waited with running engines. Fifty Jews at a time were transported to a section of Skridlevo, past the military barracks to a small clearing. This continued throughout the day.

When the sun finally set, 4,000 dead Jews lay under frozen blankets of blood at the bottom of a pit. I don't know how we escaped. All I know is that we weren't there to be counted. I'm sure it was my father's doing. He knew when we had to run and when it was safe to return. The Jews who survived Black Monday built the ghetto in Pereshike.

For four months, our family avoided the ghetto. My father found Polish peasants who would take us in, not out of love or moral responsibility but because they profited from the exchange. Sometimes our family hid together. Once my parents left me alone with a neighbor. I sat in a corner smelling bacon cook on the fire. The smell made me sick. When my parents finally retrieved me, I yelled, "Don't you ever leave me alone again. I'm staying with you!"

The concept of survival at any cost did not interest me. Without my parents, life was meaningless, even repugnant. Their love held my world together. My life was like a spider's web, precarious and unpredictable. Before the war, it was well constructed, protected. After the Nazis came, one broken thread and the entire web could collapse. So many times I was just hanging in the air: in the fields, in the forest, in so many unbelievable situations.

A Polish neighbor who wanted our property finally betrayed us to the Nazis. One night there was a loud, insistent knocking on the front door. Men in grey uniforms with thick belts and tight lips told us we had to report to the ghetto the following day. We could take only a few possessions. All I wanted was my doll. She was maybe six or seven inches tall and wore a pretty green dress my mother had sewn. I just wanted that doll.

We waited with our knapsacks that morning. I searched

my parents' eyes for reassurance. They gave me what they could — smiles and gentle words of love. Mama caught her tears quickly to prevent me from seeing them.

The Nazis came for us at the appointed time. It was warm outside. My parents stared straight ahead, each footstep dragging them further from home. Mama held Grandmother's wrinkled hand. Isaac bobbed up and down on my father's shoulders, laughing at the trees and rabbits.

I clutched my doll and tried to regulate my breathing. Jews had survived centuries of suffering. Maybe, just maybe, it would be all right. If we said nothing and did what the Nazis told us, eventually they might leave us alone. Then I could sleep in my own bed again.

As we trudged toward our destination in the dimming sunlight, I smiled bravely at Mama and squeezed Papa's fingers. He reciprocated the gesture and occasionally fluffed my hair. But his mind was miles away.

I now realize that he had glimpsed something beyond his wildest fears. It was the future, and we were nowhere to be found. When we reached the Novogrudek Ghetto, he was already planning our escape.

'One Bullet Will Quiet Us Both'

The Novogrudek Ghetto had no color. Only later did I associate this eerie vacuum with missing children. The few children who escaped the 1941 massacre and came to the ghetto were routinely slaughtered. The Nazis chased and hunted them, caught their wriggling bodies and dragged them to the forests.

Sometimes when I played out back with Isaac I thought I heard tiny voices screaming at eternity. Women gathered in small circles and wept. Others spoke in sad voices about the dead. But there was no shrieking, no wailing.

The story of one little girl circulated through the ghetto like a Yiddish folktale. When the Nazis came to shoot the girl, she held her little brother and said, "Don't worry, don't cry. One little bullet will quiet us both." I couldn't get that story out of my head, for I too had a younger brother. Will I be as brave as that faceless girl when the Nazis come for me?

I can see the decrepit buildings, the cramped room we shared with strangers, the strip of dead grass where I played. My parents tried their best to convert madness into an acceptable routine. My father reported for his job (work detail) every day. My mother invented chores to divert our empty stomachs and restlessness. Even in hell, children can get bored.

If our claustrophobia threatened the fragile peace, she let us go outside and play in the alley behind the apartment. "Don't make any noise," she implored. "Stay out of sight. And take care of your brother!" I felt her nervous, watchful eyes pierce us from the window like nails. Other kids sporadically joined us in a game of hopscotch or hide and seek until they too disappeared. Then Isaac and I were alone — two flecks of paint on a barren canvas.

One day my mother asked me to sit next to her on the small bed. "If anything happens to me or your father, promise me you will take care of Isaac." Her voice is lost to me, but I will never forget the enormity of her words. How could I be my brother's keeper? My mother waited for my answer. Stretching my arms around her thin waist, I nodded my head. "I promise, Mama. I promise."

I was just a child, vacillating between supreme confidence and abject terror. Actually, my behavior was remarkably brazen. Sometimes after Jewish families were herded into trucks, I snuck into their vacant houses. I didn't really think about what happened to those people, only what I might discover among the ruins.

My father had been sneaking undetected in and out of the ghetto for months. I had no idea where he went or why, only that I missed him horribly. But he always returned with inventive escape plans.

Papa also warned us of massacres and "selections," when the Nazis ordered Jews to pack and led them away, presumably to their deaths. I will never know how my father obtained this information, but his predictions always came true. We lived, while so many Jews died.

Our first escape occurred at night. My mother, who decided to stay behind with my sick grandmother, handed us over the ghetto wall to my father. I walked for hours, maybe all night, in fields undulating with strange sounds. Exhausted, we rested in the grass until my father roused us. I don't think he slept at all.

As dawn approached, I recognized the surroundings. "Papa, our home is right over the hill!" My expression must have cut his heart. "We can't go home, Paula. Not yet." He tied a tarp to a big tree and helped us crawl underneath.

"I'm going to find food. Watch Isaac. Be quiet. And don't worry." It was very cold. I clung to Isaac and a blanket Papa had left us for warmth. Afternoon passed into evening. I felt the stars, but I didn't want to see them. Finally I fell asleep.

I woke up early the next morning. Papa wasn't back. I cried myself to sleep. When I opened my eyes, Papa stood over me. "I told you I would return," he said as he stroked my hair. I was deliriously happy.

A day or two later our empty stomachs started rumbling. My father led us to a potato field, arranged the tarp and helped us inside again. "Don't squirm. Don't make noise. And watch Isaac." He kissed my nose and went to find food.

The hours hung motionless like injured birds confined to their nest. Purple twilight mixed with green. It was so dark, so cold. Isaac curled into my body and slept. I envied his oblivion. Invisible animals hissed and growled in the tall field. "Come back, Papa," I whispered. "Please, please, come back."

Around midday, my exhausted, elated father arrived with gifts of bread and cheese. "Eat," he said, erasing the worry from my cheeks. "It's safe now. We can go back to the ghetto. Your mother is waiting for us."

I frequently doubted God, but I never once doubted my father. This time, hundreds of children had disappeared. As soon as Mama saw us, she bit her lip to stifle her joy. The faint taste of blood lingered in her kisses.

The next time my father learned of a selection, we went to another ghetto, Dvorets. I was there for two weeks. I slept in the upper wooden bunk, and Isaac was below me. One night I had to go to the bathroom. I climbed down very carefully in the darkness. When I reached the bottom I had no idea where the bathroom was, so I climbed back up and wet the bed. I slept with bedbugs. They bit me and had the vilest smell. Lice spawned in my hair. The minute my father got wind of a selection at Dvorets, we fled.

The night we escaped Dvorets was extremely bright. Moonlight shivered on the pitch-black swamp in the potato field. At some point we had to cross a railroad track. Above us, Nazis marched on a bridge. They stomped their boots in some sinister dance, their guns glistening like daggers. More than 70 years later, that memory is as sharp as steel.

My father told us to hide in the underbrush. I was trapped. One wrong move, one audible whimper, and my life would be over. Somehow, I did not fall off the edge of the world. My father slipped us inside the Novogrudek ghetto just in time. Years later I found out that Dvorets was liquidated in December of 1942. The Nazis executed 10,000 men, women and children at an undisclosed location.

Almost every Jew in the Novogrudek ghetto had heard astonishing tales of the Bielski partisans and their victories in the Naliboki forest in Belarus. Tuvia, Zus and their younger brother Asael Bielski sought sanctuary in the forest shortly after their parents were killed in the Novogrudek massacre of 1941. Their initial encampment consisted of relatives and friends.

As our situation deteriorated, Tuvia (now commander of the partisans) scaled our ghetto walls to convince people to join him. "We are your only chance," he pleaded at secret meetings. Relying on rumors instead of maps, Jews with nothing to lose set out on the journey toward doubtful salvation. Many died in the process.

The very young don't attach despair to a specific date. Since

I could not tell time or track its passage, I don't know when Papa joined the Bielski partisans. He did not say goodbye, at least to me. Depression followed me everywhere like a faithful companion.

My mother constantly reassured me that my father loved us above all else and would never abandon us. "Be patient," she soothed. "Have faith. Papa is trying to find a good home for us outside the ghetto so we can leave this terrible place."

I'm positive my father tried to get word to us during those intolerable months, but there were no letters, no notes or communication of any kind. Although Mama pretended everything would be fine, her mounting insecurity clawed the walls. The Nazis were getting hungry. Impending slaughter dripped in the air.

I felt like a sitting duck in a poisoned pond, suspended between life and death. I could no longer remember hope.

The Wheel of My Life

By the summer of 1942, my father had been gone so long I couldn't summon his face. Children have short memories. And despite her valiant efforts to cheer us, my mother was getting desperate. I finally admitted to myself, if not out loud to Mama, that my father might be dead.

Like my mother, I cried when I was alone. Isaac, protected by his age, delighted in childish pleasures. I helped Mama with chores and played with Isaac in the alley out back. That's where I was when the Nazis tore her from my life forever.

The Polish man who wanted our property was aware of my father's unexplained absences from the ghetto. Motivated by greed and hatred, he informed on my father to the ghetto authorities.

I was outside playing. When I came upstairs, Mama was gone. My aunt told me that the Nazis stormed our building shouting my father's name and Mama dropped her sewing.

"Where is your husband?" My mother said she didn't know. "Where is your husband?" She said he left her months ago. "Where are your children?" She said she had no children. The Nazis pushed her down the stairs to the truck below.

No one saw her again. One of my cousins later told me that my mother had tears in her eyes when she looked at my aunt for the last time. Death had found her at last.

I fully expected to see Mama when I returned to our rooms after playing in the alley. But she was gone. My aunt tried to comfort me: "Your mother has been arrested but she'll probably be back soon."

"Soon" was meaningless in the ghetto. Once the Nazis took you, it was all over. Exterminating us was their ultimate goal. I stopped asking about my mother, because I knew she was dead. My mother was the wheel of my life. Without her, my world stopped turning. There was no one to comfort me or sustain illusions of happy endings. If I could have willed myself to go to sleep and never wake up, I would have gladly done it.

It was early fall. The dreadful news of my mother's arrest reached my father, who was finalizing our escape route to the Naliboki woods. The Nazis do not let people go free. They execute them. Papa realized his children were next.

The exact timing eludes me, but late one night a stranger woke me from a deep sleep. "You and your brother must dress quickly," he said. "I am taking you to meet a farmer. Do what he tells you, and be silent as the grave. I know that what I ask of you is frightening, but your father is waiting on the other side. It's now or never."

A Polish farmer my father trusted was responsible for wheeling barrels of water into the ghetto for the Nazis. This time, after emptying the barrels, he cautiously whispered our names. I grabbed Isaac's hand and rushed to the farmer, who pushed us inside one of the barrels. He stuffed a torn blanket beneath us, sealed the lid and placed it on his horse-drawn carriage. To avoid discovery, we stayed in that dank coffin for endless hours. I held Isaac tightly in my arms so he wouldn't start crying.

Just when I thought I couldn't take one more second, the carriage stopped. The farmer opened the barrel and gently extricated us. He led us to a dry barn, helped us up to the hayloft and fed us hardboiled eggs, dark bread and water.

All night I imagined seeing Papa again. Sleep was impossible. At the same time, I was mature enough to grasp the odds. What if something happened? Poles received a tidy sum for turning over Jews to the Nazis. Any second I could be shot, and my dreams would die with me. I wanted so much to talk to Isaac, but he slept like a baby.

The next morning, the farmer carved a deep hole in the back of the wagon, told us to hide inside and covered it with hay. My 20-year-old cousin Dashke, who escaped from the ghetto about the same time we did, was at the farmhouse. She sat in the front seat of the wagon. Wearing a traditional peasant's scarf, she pretended to be the farmer's wife.

Around twilight, the carriage stopped at a remote farmhouse in the forest. My father, ashen and overwhelmed, picked us up in his arms. Our sentences overlapped, as did our sorrow. We wept for a courageous wife and mother who went to her death in our place. I heard that 2,000 Jews from the Novogrudek ghetto were massacred around the time of our escape. I only thought of Mama.

Much later in the forest, I overheard new refugees from Novogrudek discussing Mama. She did not die immediately. The Nazis used her as a translator for six weeks before killing her.

Mama was murdered in September of 1942, on Yom Kippur, the Day of Atonement. I can only envision her final hours: trembling alone on a crowded truck, kneeling over hundreds of lifeless bodies, a bullet destroying her brain. Beyond that, I cannot go.

No matter how strong the love, death severs the physical connection. But the love never goes away. In my child's mind, I always hoped that my mother would turn up somewhere. That thought persisted for many years, even though I knew it was impossible. I hoped against hope that she would show up. But she never did.

I went on a mission to Poland in 1999 with Rabbi Stanley Wagner, the longtime rabbi at our synagogue in Denver. We toured many sites, including a mass grave in Ponar, near Vilna. The Nazis murdered thousands of Jews in Ponar and threw their bodies into a fathomless pit. This is how my mother died.

Over the decades, the residents of Ponar attempted to cover up the graves — but they kept sinking deeper in the earth. All the birds left that forest, driven out by the smell of burned and rotting flesh. They have not returned.

My mother is not buried in Ponar. I will never find her grave. But wherever she is, I hope flowers grow and the birds are not afraid to sing.

Waking Up in the Forest

My father held the reins of the horse-drawn cart, which rambled along a tangled path. A quilt of stars lit the moonless night. Our little trio barely spoke. Papa was silent. Isaac slept on my lap in the front seat, occasionally sniveling under the blanket. I rested my head on my father's shoulder. Trees swished and swayed, emitting a heavy pine scent.

Blackness obscured the landscape. I couldn't really see anything — yet I sensed something immense rising around me. The feeling was so powerful that the hair on the back of my neck stood up, but not out of fear. I felt like I belonged to something much greater than myself.

With Papa beside me, I was content to stay like this forever. This mysterious night wrapped us inside a miracle — fragile, temporary, but a miracle while it lasted. You didn't ask for more. Just when I started to nod off, my father pinched my arm gently and pointed to a campfire in the distance. I could hear people's voices. "Wake up, Paula," he said. "This is your new home."

As we strolled through the curious group, bodies parted

like the Reed Sea. Men blinked away tears and congratulated my father. Mothers regarded us with visible pain because they knew their own children were lost to them. Isaac laughed, extending his arms to all the women. Some turned away from him.

My father opened a tent-like covering, spread a blanket on the ground and told us to keep each other warm. He stayed up talking to the men but the nearness of his voice lulled me to sleep. For the first time in recent memory, nightmares did not visit me. When a chilly finger of air nudged me awake, Isaac clapped his hands. I'd never seen him so excited.

My father motioned for us to sit with him on a log. A woman said hello in Yiddish and handed me a hot, sweet drink and warm bread. Birds chirped in the damp mist. I burrowed myself into my father, whose mood was ebullient, and peered beyond the fog. What I couldn't hear or see — soldiers, barking dogs, barbed wire fences — told me every-thing. I was free.

This beautiful place resembled an etching in one of my cousin's storybooks, where fairy queens inhabited the tree-tops and mothers lived forever. But I was too old for fantasies.

My mother was dead, and I did not believe in fairies or God. When my father turned to me, he froze. An older, despairing soul had claimed his little daughter. I looked the same, but something inside me had changed forever. I knew too much. And now he knew it too.

A magnificent horse interrupted our thoughts. Straddling the chestnut-hued animal was a statuesque, handsome man with wavy dark hair, a mustache and shiny boots. My father rushed over to him. "Tuvia, meet my children!"

Dismounting his horse, Commander Tuvia Bielski shook my brother's tiny hand. "You must be Isaac, named after Abraham's son. Isaac is one of the three patriarchs in Judaism. He was almost sacrificed on Mount Moriah, but God had another plan for him — and you too, I suspect." Isaac just blinked his eyes. "And this is my daughter Paula," my father said, inching me forward. Tuvia kissed my hand. "You are the smart one, am I right? Wolf, you forgot to tell me how pretty she is." "Being smart is more important than being pretty," I countered. Tuvia threw his head back and laughed. "Yes, you are right about that." Even off his horse, Tuvia Bielski was a giant of a man.

Fall was beautiful in the forest. I had never seen such magnificent colors. As the nights grew frosty, dew-speckled moss, grass and leaves greeted me every morning. The artist in me began studying nature: how a slice of blue sky split and slipped through the pine trees; a green spinning wheel painting the bushes; the wet texture of leaves glistening in the sunshine. Whenever I forgot the hateful world that brought me to this place, I appreciated the Naliboki's beauty.

Hundreds of Jews dwelled in the dense forest, including countless women who had lost their husbands and children. These women gravitated toward men who could offer them protection. If a man accepted a woman as his companion, she became his forest wife. These mutually supportive alliances would not be tolerated in traditional Jewish society, but there was nothing traditional about our circumstances.

Papa had several admirers. Not long after he took me to the Naliboki, a woman named Rivka tried to ingratiate herself with me. She brought me hot chocolate and introduced herself. That simple, suggestive act infuriated me. I pushed the drink away and it landed on her clothes. "I don't need another mother," I yelled. Apparently, she didn't need me either. I never saw her again.

It's true I had discovered a sanctuary of sorts in the Naliboki. On good days, life obeyed a pragmatic, almost peaceful rhythm. I studied Hebrew with Papa and participated in age-appropriate activities. There were no other children to talk to except Isaac, and his vocabulary was extremely limited.

One morning I opened the tent to a white wonderland of snow. Winter had arrived. My father joined the men in building *zemylankas*, or log bunkers. Built deep into the cold earth, they were accessible by ladders made of tree branches. Once I told my father that I wanted to try my hand at chopping wood. How difficult could it be? He put a piece of wood on a tree stump, gave me a small axe and observed me from a cautious distance. I never offered my services again.

As the months passed and I grew taller, the sleeves on my little blue coat reached my elbows. For shoes I wrapped rags around my feet and tied them with string. This was not a luxury camp in the Catskills or the Wisconsin countryside. Yes, we enjoyed a taste of freedom, but it was temporary and conditional. Death always lurked over our shoulders. The partisans were not alone in the Naliboki. Anti-Semitic Poles and rogue Soviet partisans also hunted in that forest, and not just for food. They hunted Jews.

Papa dedicated his entire being to keeping us safe. He never discussed it with me, but I think he was haunted by guilt. The Nazis could not find my father so they arrested my mother. Then they killed her. Just as I promised that I would take care of Isaac if anything happened to her, I have always believed that my father made the same promise.

He refused to volunteer for dangerous military attacks in the forest even though he burned to fight. *Malbushim* (literally "clothes") was a derogatory Yiddish term for useless individuals. Wolf Koladicki was not a *malbush*. He was a brave man who would go to any lengths to keep us alive.

Papa volunteered for food missions. Far less dangerous than blowing up bridges, it was still a risky enterprise. We lived in a forest infested with enemies. He carried a German Luger, although he rarely used it. Tuvia ordered the partisans to demand enough food to survive but to refrain from greed. Some Poles obliged willingly. Others handed over the food, waited until it was safe and then contacted the Nazis. Gunfights ensued. Men were killed.

One night my father didn't come back with the others. As I repeated his name in the night, I overheard people talking about Isaac and me. If something happened to my father, they said we would probably be killed. I was horrified. How could this be? The cruel answer was based in logic.

My father adhered to the partisan code, designed to ensure the group's survival. The partisans had to run at a moment's notice. Children, especially ones as young as we were, slowed them down. As long as Papa lived, we lived. If he died, we died. Our mother was gone. Without Papa, we would be alone — and potentially compromise everyone's safety.

Papa needed a woman to care for his children. It didn't take long to find her. Chana was small, frail and somber. The Nazis had murdered her husband and children. After spending time together, my father and Chana became a couple. I know she loved Papa. That's why she promised to watch over us. Otherwise Papa would have never consented to the relationship. But she never loved me. Whenever he was away, I felt desperately alone.

In retrospect, I understand Chana's inability to love a child that was not her own. I could not replace her children. She could not replace my mother. Still, in all the years that Chana lived with us — throughout the war, after liberation, in the displaced persons camp and Chicago — my stepmother never once hugged or kissed me.

I experienced many deprivations in the Naliboki, but Chana was the coldest comfort of all.

Kaddish for the Dead and the Living

That first howling winter in the Naliboki lasted for so many months I wondered if I would ever see spring again. I still loved the billowing snow, a revolving wheel of pinks and purples depending on the hour. It covered our tracks, protected us from invaders, and dictated our movements. When storms struck with blinding rage, we scattered to parts unknown, leaving the little we had accumulated behind. The Bielski partisans did not sleep underneath the same constellations night after night, for we were rarely in one place longer than a month. Still, Jews continued arriving at our camp in huddled clusters. And we were happy to see them.

Our group stayed with Tuvia Bielski unless circumstances separated us. When we split up, several people regularly accompanied my father, confident he would lead them to safety. Papa was a human compass. Out of ten potential alternatives, he invariably chose the right direction. And in that first sign of spring, when ice dripped from the trees, we always met up with Tuvia Bielski again.

For Isaac, the Naliboki was a tantalizing zoo. While Papa taught him to distinguish between harmless and dangerous animals, Isaac believed in the goodness of all creatures. One day my father gave Isaac a small chick. Isaac was so happy — he finally met a playmate his age. He trained that chick, even taught it to fly. Then we ran out of food and Isaac's pet became our dinner. Despite the war and his mother's death, losing that chick to hunger seemed like the cruelest punishment.

Another time, Isaac disappeared. He usually sat by the entrance to our *zemylanka*, chattering to trees and squirrels. But when we called his name he wasn't there. I joined the search party, sliding on the ice-packed earth as freezing flakes of snow stung my eyes. We could not find him anywhere.

Wolves prowled around our bunker. With each passing minute, I imagined a wolf shaking Isaac's lifeless body with its bloody teeth. Finally we spotted him in the distance, safe in his little coat and hat, singing a Russian song. Some endings are kinder than others.

Every time my father left on a food mission, severe anxiety incapacitated me. I couldn't eat, I couldn't move. No matter how hard Papa tried to reassure me that we'd see each other again, I covered my ears. "You won't come back," I yelled. "And I will die." Each time he headed into the unknown, my fear walked with him.

I should have been strong for his sake. He loved me so much! Instead my courage turned to dust. Sleep, my only refuge, beckoned like a drug. If I was lucky, the morning would forget me. And if I was very lucky, Papa would kiss me awake.

My father constantly went on food missions for potatoes, onions, bread, buttermilk — anything remotely fit for human consumption. The challenge was maintaining a steady food supply from Polish farmers in the region, which became increasingly difficult. First, the Poles needed to feed their own families. And those who were willing to help in the beginning now informed on us to the Nazis.

Early one morning, Papa and five other men set off with canvas bags swinging from their shoulders and guns tucked into their waists. That evening we heard rumors of a skirmish between the Nazis and five Bielski partisans. "Three of our men are dead," one woman wailed. "No, four," corrected another. Without witnesses, they indulged in wild speculation. By the time the stars telegraphed one another in the sky, my father had not returned.

I lapsed into a comatose state and retreated to a corner of our bunker. I don't know how many days I stayed like this. The people in our bunker must have taken turns giving me water to sip. My memories are blurry.

But I was convinced that if I didn't move, death would catch me like an animal in a trap. And each day that death ignored me, I cursed God for letting me live. From what I had seen, death was not the worst thing that awaited me. Living was the real hell.

About five days later I heard my father singing. He had an unmistakable voice, sonorous and beautiful. I thought I was dreaming but the sound grew louder and louder. When Papa ran into the bunker and lifted me from my straw bed, I screamed — out of shock or joy or both.

It was no secret that an anti-Semitic band of Russian partisans coveted my father's gun. One night as Papa was cleaning his Luger outside the bunker, a roving and very drunk gang of Soviet partisans snuck up on him and started shooting.

It was so dark they hit everything except my father. We saw the bullet holes in the trees the next morning. But Papa had escaped deeper into the forest. He was afraid the Russians might return and endanger the camp. This time he vanished for more than a month.

While I was immune to most illnesses that affected the partisans, including stomach disorders, I finally succumbed to a horrible skin malady that looked like leprosy. Isaac caught it too. When my father saw us after a five-week absence, he broke down and sobbed.

Our fingers stuck together like glue, and pus-filled sores disfigured our hands. We hadn't bathed in a while, and it's probable we suffered from malnutrition. A friend of my father's suggested the only remedy was a disinfecting bath. Papa sprang into action.

Using a makeshift sleigh, my father wrapped us inside mountains of blankets and stopped at the first farmhouse with a light burning in the window. A Polish woman answered the door. She stared at us — two Jewish children and a frantic father — then motioned us inside. My father showed her our hands. "My children need a bath," he pleaded.

The woman pulled out a wooden tub normally reserved for laundry. Papa filled it with adult urine, the only available disinfectant. Then the woman gave him some lard, which he massaged into our hands to pry apart our fingers.

When we were ready to leave, the woman pressed a jar of lard into my father's hands. Long after the sores disappeared, I wondered about that woman, and whether her light continued to burn.

My father taught me many things in the forest: the complexity of checkers and the excitement of jumping to victory; how to find the direction "north" by studying moss on the trees; the Russian and Hebrew alphabet; stories that fed my imagination and soothed my slumber.

And he was always talking about my mother — her beauty, brilliance and compassion. The first Hebrew prayer he taught me was the *Kaddish*, the Jewish prayer for the dead. I think Papa wanted me to be able to recite the *Kaddish* for him, in case he was killed. Most importantly, he made sure I said it to calm my mother's restless soul.

What Dreams May Come

One night, a doubled-up figure hurried by me in the bunker. The next night, two people ran outside. Given the damp chill and our impoverished diet, stomach maladies were common. Before I knew it, everyone was sick except for our family and a few others. It was typhus, and it raged in epidemic proportions. Nonsensical words oozed from fever-parched lips like unintelligible prophecies. A strange rash reddened pallid faces.

Although Isaac and I felt fine, my father initiated a list of safety instructions to protect against contagion. He made me stay inside our bunker more than usual. I could still venture outside, but only long enough to observe the mood around me.

Couples held each other close. Abject loneliness embraced women without partners. Vigorous men wilted under stones of fatigue.

I always assumed a single, well-aimed bullet would kill me, like that little girl in the ghetto. Typhus took its time. Most of the partisans survived, but many rotted under unblessed mounds of earth.

I never had much of an appetite, even when I was starving. Fear cancels out hunger. Every day my father insisted I eat his food. "You must stay healthy for me," he urged. He even indulged in pantomime to stimulate my interest. Rubbing his cold hands together, Papa would make a face and hold a bite of stale bread to his nose. "It's just like Mama's *challah*!" he winked. I chewed an obligatory piece and gave the rest to Isaac, who devoured it.

Bunkers typically accommodated up to 40 people. During the epidemic, Papa received permission to build a separate bunker to minimize the risk of contagion. My family, which included Chana, shared this new living quarter with Mordechai and his wife Lotte, Berel Lifshitz and his wife, and Lifshitz' father.

The elder Mr. Lifshitz went to the U.S. before World War II but he didn't like it. He loved telling us fascinating and funny stories about life in New York. I vaguely remember Lotte because she was so fond of me. "Paula is such a beautiful child," she often said. Lotte always asked Isaac what he wanted to eat because she adored his answer: "*A bisl essen!*

Anything!" Our family came through the epidemic unscathed.

Erecting a *zemylanka* was a collaborative effort. After felling trees, the men dug large holes in the ground, filled the bottom with straw and logs, stacked interlocking poles for walls and stuffed empty spaces with tree branches. But the bunkers provided more than mere shelter from the elements. In the event that our enemies discovered us, each *zemylanka* contained a secondary hiding compartment. We would be safe there, provided we had advance warning.

One night my father fell asleep on patrol duty. My mother appeared to him in a dream: "Wolf, wake up. Wake up! You must get back to the children or they will die!" Mama screamed this warning repeatedly in his sleep. Papa ran and ran yet his legs never moved. Papa flailed wildly in the dream against some spectral force. My mother's voice rose to a terrifying pitch: "*Wulfe*, hurry and get the children!"

He woke up and sprinted toward the bunker. He climbed inside and pushed everyone inside the tunnel. Just as we slid the door behind us, boots trampled over our straw beds. German soldiers barked frantic orders during their futile search. Finally they left.

The partisans attributed our narrow escape, and all the ones before and after, to Wolf Koladicki's second sight. Perhaps that's one of the reasons they revered and trusted him so much. Papa and I never spoke about it. I don't think he understood it either. To me, his gifts were miraculous. Still, I placed my faith in luck, not miracles. One spring afternoon, as my father washed my lice-infested braids in the river, I couldn't contain my skepticism. "Did Mama really talk to you that night you fell asleep on patrol? Was she happy?"

Averting his face, he looked up at hundreds of birds migrating across the horizon. "It was a dream," he said, "and as real as this moment. This is not the life I planned for my family. I was born under a dark star. If we ever come through this, I will offer a prayer of gratitude to God. But before I thank God, I will thank your mother." Now it was my turn to stare at the birds. I did not want to drown Papa in my tears.

A few weeks later, a Russian plane transporting supplies to Soviet partisans landed in our encampment. Feeling courageous, I spoke to the pilots. "Come with us to Moscow," they offered, obviously impressed with my Russian. The men were nice, but "nice" had no currency in the Holocaust. The Russian partisans, many of whom respected the Bielski brothers, could never forget they were Jews. Although we fought the same enemy, the Russians regarded us as inferior beings. I could only trust my family, the Commander and a few acquaintances. The world was a duplicitous web.

Still, childish curiosity tempted me to hop on the rickety plane. In the end it didn't matter. Papa adamantly withheld his permission. "If you go with them you are lost," he said, "to me and to yourself."

Eventually the reprieves — warmer weather, a good night's sleep that lasted well into the morning, unremarkable days — no longer consoled me. They were nothing more than a mirage, a moment's peace wedged between the chaos. We were constantly pursued in this ghetto without walls. A different kind of cage, it was still a formidable prison.

My only crime was being born a Jew. For that reason alone, I was forced to live like an animal. On a relative scale, many equate the partisan way of life with a less tortuous passage through the Holocaust. They are mistaken. I never expected to come out of the Naliboki alive.

One day my father collapsed while sawing trees for a bunker. I was playing checkers with Lufka, a 19-year-old boy who idolized Papa, when we heard the commotion. "Something has happened to Wolf," voices murmured in disbelief. "He's fainted. Get help!" Though I was only a few yards away, I ran so fast my heart nearly exploded. Then I saw Papa stretched lifeless on the snow, his face drained bluish white.

Before I could touch him, Chana pushed me aside and grabbed my father's shoulders. "*Wulfe*, what is wrong? Dear God, he's burning up! Find the doctor!" Two or three men carried Papa to the nearest bunker and lowered him on a makeshift table. I was left behind.

I snuck inside the bunker with Lufka, who gently maneuvered me to the front. The doctor — probably in his early 40's, the same age as my father — examined Papa with methodical urgency. "His breathing is shallow and his pulse is weak," he announced. As the anxious minutes passed, the doctor could not hide his bewilderment. Then he turned Papa over on his back, revealing a blistering angry-red wound. The room gasped.

"What is this?" I demanded, drawing unwanted attention.

"Be quiet little girl," the doctor snapped. "Don't you let my father die!" I yelled. The doctor paid no attention. There wasn't time.

At some point he injected penicillin into Papa, who fell violently ill. No one had any idea that he was allergic to penicillin. Chana cringed fearfully. I held out my hand to her but she pushed it away.

Lufka tapped me on the shoulder and motioned for me to leave. "Your father wouldn't want you to watch this," he whispered. "He would want you to pray. Come outside with me."

A fresh band of spring snow encircled us. Lufka knelt in prayer and folded his fingers together. Hebrew words flew from his mouth like a strange species of butterflies. I refused to pray. God had abandoned us. Besides, the only prayer Papa taught me was the *Kaddish*. I was not ready to give up.

I loved my father more than life. And I knew, one way or another, that my life would end with his. Ever since I heard people talking about Isaac and me around the campfire, I carried this secret around like a bullet in my soul. I didn't blame anyone. I was nine. Isaac was four. The Bielskis could not risk the lives of hundreds of Jews to save two children.

My father hung suspended between life and death for weeks and weeks. I visited as often as the doctor allowed. The rest of the time I kept close to Isaac, who thought Papa was out looking for food again. Chana did not leave my father. Observant Jews recited prayers for a *refuah shl'ema*, a complete recovery. The religiously disinclined held him in their thoughts. Life's fragility was the one irrefutable fact that united us.

One spring morning, good fortune took pity on my beloved dark star. He said my name, stretched out his arms and wrapped me in smiles. In a rare reversal of roles, he let me feed him broth. The wooden spoon trembled as I held it in my hands. "Taste this, Papa. It's just like Mama's chicken soup!"

I didn't remember her chicken soup. Papa knew this. Still, he sipped the broth and nodded. We both pretended, out of love. "You're right," he said. "It's exactly like Mama's."

'And Abraham Raised His Knife'

The Bielski partisans blew up bridges, sabotaged Nazi installations and executed Polish traitors. I don't know how many actual fighters we had, but like the mouse that roared, the Bielskis sustained the illusion that we were a massive threat. Tuvia Bielski was a chameleon of mythic proportions, altering his personality to accomplish his ends. The Soviet partisans simultaneously dreaded and admired him.

We loved Tuvia because he was our Moses, prolonging our fragile days so we might taste freedom again. Tuvia was the ideal Jewish leader: handsome, charismatic, strong, invincible. I was incapable of separating the man from the legend. His private heart was a foreign country few were allowed to visit, which heightened his appeal to the opposite sex. The fact that so many women wanted to keep company with him was the worst kept secret in the forest.

In July of 1943, our transient peace collapsed. The Nazis, intent on annihilating the Bielski partisans, issued an official document outlining their plan of attack. Debilitated and cornered on all fronts, tempers erupted in angry staccatos.

Papa constantly reassured me that Tuvia would pull another miracle out of his leather cap, but I knew he was very worried.

As the Nazi ambushes accelerated and we still lacked an exit strategy, Tuvia felt like he was drowning on dry land. In our years in the Naliboki, it was not uncommon for the dissatisfied among us to defy his authority. Tuvia was our commander. He anticipated dissention and skillfully controlled it. Now his fury teetered on the irrational. Tuvia threatened anyone who challenged him with exile — the equivalent of a death sentence. Our hero was human after all.

Asael Bielski coordinated large-scale food missions in order to shore up our meager supplies. Each time Papa accompanied Asael on these interminable journeys beyond the camp, Chana ignored me. I heard her tell the women, "I am not the mother of Wolf's children. My children are dead."

Michal Mechlis, a land surveyor in his previous life, and Akiva Szymonowic, who had also worked in the Naliboki, finally came up with a radical, almost inconceivable idea. We would cross the Naliboki *Puscha*, a big wetland swamp, to the remote island of Krasnaya Gorka.

The journey would last about seven days. Tuvia agreed to

the plan, explaining that the Nazis would not risk following us. He addressed the entire camp — more than a thousand Jews — and said that this was our only way out.

The night before our journey, the men gulped *Somagonka*, the moonshine of the forest, and sang partisan songs in Yiddish under the full moon. Tuvia sat alone on a ridge, absorbed in his thoughts. Papa avoided looking at Isaac and me. What was he asking his children to do? He dulled his doubts with uncharacteristic swigs of the potent alcohol.

We got up before dawn and made our way to the swamp. When we arrived at the edges, Isaac and I were put at the front of the long, nervous line. Papa stayed with us. Armed men and women brought up the rear. I held Papa's hand and Isaac straddled his shoulders. My friend Lufka was right behind us.

Tuvia repeatedly warned the children that silence was indispensable to our survival. If we made too much noise the Nazis would follow us. I rubbed my finger over my lips, gluing them with imaginary paste. Isaac was irritable and disoriented. I was afraid he might cry. But Isaac loved Papa's shoulders more than any place in the world. He fell asleep.

We waded deeper and deeper into the swamp. The cold dirty water reached my neck. I couldn't stop shivering. Papa kissed my forehead and tried to warm my chattering teeth with stories. I dragged one exhausted foot in front of the other but I never seemed to move. The water pinned my legs in murky chains.

Interminable days ran together. How long had we been out here? Sometimes the swamp covered my mouth. I wanted to stop. Papa grabbed me. "Keep going," he pleaded. "Keep going." I got so tired I slept standing up. My father searched for a resting place. Out of nowhere he glimpsed a tiny strip of land. "Can you see that?" he gestured excitedly. "We'll stay there for a bit."

We reached an elevated mound of dry dirt, slithered out of the swamp and collapsed. Papa comforted our fatigue in his soaking arms. While he and I tried to sleep, Isaac ate some moldy kernels he discovered in a decrepit chicken coop. His playful chatter kept disrupting our rest but we all finally slept. I don't know how long we were out, but when we opened our eyes we were horrified. The partisans were nowhere in sight.

"Where is everyone?" I screamed, breaking the code of

silence. "I don't know," my father said. "I don't know." Papa lifted Isaac on his shoulder, grabbed my wrist and together we scrambled back into the swamp. At first I moved quickly, until the water gradually slowed my legs. "We are lost, Papa. We are dead." "We are not dead, but we are lost," Papa said. "We'll find them."

God created the world in seven days. The Bielski partisans endured seven days in that hellish swamp. When they finally arrived at Krasnaya Gorka, they counted heads. Six people were missing — including Wolf Koladicki and his two children. Tuvia sent out a search party to rescue us. It was an act of desperation, and commitment.

I was the first to see them — three or four men trudging through the swamp, their guns bouncing on their shoulders. "We're here, we're here!" I waved. My father started shouting. Even Isaac, whose stomach had been bothering him, brightened up. We did not move an inch, lest one wrong move separate us from life.

The partisans were overjoyed. "Here you are! Thank God! Thank God!" they murmured. Having no use for God, I thanked the partisans instead. Singing triumphant, off-key melodies, they escorted us to Krasnaya Gorka.

Isaac couldn't recover from those kernels he devoured in the chicken coup. They expanded inside him, distending his belly and inflicting intolerable pain. Wailing at the top of his lungs, Isaac begged my father to cut open his stomach and remove the poison. "Poor little boy," some people sympathized. Others squirmed apprehensively: "If your son keeps this up, he'll lead the enemy right to us."

Since it was July, we slept under tents. Everyone could hear Isaac's continual groans. Papa assuaged his son with all his paternal might. The doctor applied medicinal concoctions. Nothing worked.

(I had repressed the following until I heard the tape my niece recorded with Chana in the 1970s.)

Tuvia Bielski came into our tent, knelt by Isaac and stroked his forehead. My father quickly appraised the situation. "Forgive me, my dear friend," Tuvia said. "But we are near a populated area and Isaac is endangering the lives of a thousand Jews. I can't allow that. As much as it hurts me, I can't allow it."

Tuvia stood up, pulled out his gun, cocked it, and aimed

it at Isaac. Papa sprang on Isaac like a tiger, enveloping his small body. "If you kill my son, you must kill me too. Do you hear me, Tuvia? You'll have to kill us both."

Tuvia hesitated. "*Wulfe* . . ."

Papa clutched Isaac and refused to budge. Tuvia replaced the pistol in his thick belt and left our tent. He did not return for several weeks, until my brother was much better.

I'm convinced that God did not prevent Isaac's sacrifice that awful day. Papa saved Isaac's life because he was willing to sacrifice his own.

Vengeance is Ours

Krasnaya Gorka was not the Promised Land. The Nazis surrounded our little island and malnutrition spread throughout the camp. For two months, Tuvia observed us with tragic, pathetic eyes. Weakened and ill from the constant lack of food, I prepared to die. But death would not have me. Papa and the other men begged Tuvia to lead us back to the camp we abandoned for the swamp.

I preferred a quick death to slow starvation. I had seen skeletal remains in the ghetto: bones suspended in gruesome prayer, beseeching God for their final release. That wasn't for me.

Apparently, I wasn't alone. Zus Bielski assembled a scouting party of 80 men to see if we could slip through Nazi lines, and promised to send word to the *Otriad* (military unit). One day passed, then two. There was no message. Tuvia paced aimlessly. Sensing death's imminence, Papa never left us alone. It wouldn't be long before fresh graves choked on Jewish corpses.

On the third day, Tuvia gathered us together and

announced, "We are going back to our old camp near Stanke-vich." A few people complained, but I was glad. The old camp almost felt like home. Groups of twenty to thirty partisans gathered us together. I was assigned to the last contingent with Isaac and the noncombatants. Tuvia, his brother Asael, Layzer Malbin and Papa took the lead.

Signs of a diminishing Nazi presence littered the journey. I peed on crumpled packs of German cigarettes; tripped over spent German cartridges. The Nazis may have retreated from the area, but we had not escaped their hatred.

With the exception of one man who fell off his horse and drowned in the Neiman River, we all arrived safely at our destination — including Zus and the 80 men we thought were dead. I see the trees bending to welcome us, and the sky winking in recognition.

I have no idea whether I would recognize anything if I returned to the Naliboki today, yet I've often wondered whether that immense forest would remember me at all.

At some point, Papa devised a plan to kill the Pole who had stolen our ranch and was complicit in the arrest and death of my mother. My father did not share his intentions with me, or the partisans he asked to go with him.

One day I saw him speaking in hushed tones to four or five men, including my older cousin Yanek. "I need you to help me find food," Papa said. "And I have to make a stop outside Novogrudek. Are you in?" They nodded and shook hands.

That night, boisterous laughter interrupted my slumber. Many partisans drank *Somagonka* to steel their nerves before a perilous mission. I instinctively turned toward Papa's straw mattress. It was empty. Then I heard him crying outside. Something told me to leave him alone, and I fell asleep.

In the morning Papa was gone, and so was his prized revolver. As I sat around the campfire, rumors of Papa's whereabouts fanned the glowing embers. All I could do was wait.

Papa and his friends had struck out for the ranch. Yanek asked him, "Where are we going?" "I'll tell you later," Papa said evasively. In those days, conjecture blew through small towns like spring pollen. The Pole living in our property heard that Wolf Koladicki was coming for him, so he bought two ferocious dogs to alert him to trespassers.

The moment Papa and his group snuck up on the house, the animals started snarling and the man ran outside with his revolver. Gunfire was exchanged but Papa missed his target, which he later blamed on too much *Somagonka*.

Papa attacked again, this time with fire. He wrapped a kerosene-soaked rag around a stick, lit it and threw it on the porch. The other partisans fueled the fire with their torches. Our vulnerable wooden ranch crumbled to the ground. Somehow the Pole survived.

Papa returned to camp a few days later. He didn't tell me what happened at the ranch, but he was inconsolable. "I failed your mother. I failed her." I took his hand. "You didn't let Mama down," I said. "I know she's happy because we're alive. That's the only thing she wants now."

From 1943-1944, the partisans established a viable Jewish community referred to as "Jerusalem in the Woods." We had a school, an infirmary, a soap factory, metal workshop, bakery and bath house. I played games around the buildings, always with Isaac in tow.

But I never went near the tannery, where religious Jews prayed in the adjacent *shul*. Unlike some partisan accounts, I don't recall celebrating Passover in April. I believed in Papa, Tuvia and fortunate outcomes. I had seen my share of miracles. I just stopped seeing God in the miracle.

I could always judge our situation by my father's face. When worry tightened his lips, I knew we were in trouble. If he smiled, I dared to hope. Papa told me which way our wind was blowing without saying a word.

Almost 10 years old and curious to a fault, I also paid close attention to conversations around the campfire. "The Nazis are winning." "No, no, the Nazis are losing." "You'll see, the Soviet Army will save us in a matter of months." For the caged soul, freedom is a delightful obsession.

It was the beginning of the end for Nazi Germany. Chaos dismantled the German lines in Belarus. Entire divisions scattered into the unfamiliar abyss of the Naliboki. After more than two years in her majestic midst, I grew to understand my forest: her seasonal moods of frenzied snow, bone-chilling cold and generous warmth. Now the Nazis scrambled through the Naliboki like blind, frightened rabbits. What happened next was inevitable.

One morning shortly after breakfast, two young German

soldiers stumbled right into the middle of our camp. Terrified, they begged us to give them what they tried to steal from us — the chance to live. Tuvia and a few partisans interrogated the Germans. Finally they released them to unmitigated, pent up fury. Bloodlust washed the sun.

I was so small I had to push my way through a wall of bodies to get a good look. Strangely thrilled and not at all horrified, I watched people strike the soldiers with fists, sticks and rocks. "You killed my son!" one man cried. "You murdered my husband and my children!" another woman shouted. Hundreds of names and hundreds of curses assaulted the men, who succumbed to their collective punishment.

Everyone stood silently, staring at the ground. Then someone called for our two surviving horses. Obeying an unspoken directive, the animals trampled the lifeless bodies until not even God could resurrect them whole.

The crowd lingered, spent and unrepentant. Papa suddenly appeared out of nowhere and grabbed me. "Get away from here!" he ordered. "You should not see this!" He limped slightly. Sweat dripped from his forehead.

I wanted to ask him, did you kick them hard for Mama? I never did. In retrospect, some questions are better left unasked, and unanswered.

A Bed of My Own

The Russians' victories over the Germans in July of 1944 boosted morale beyond our wildest expectations. Despite these successes, the Nazis continued hunting Jews. I was not safe. None of us were safe. On July 9, a marauding group of Nazis shot their way into our camp.

Papa had just finished washing us in the river when we heard the zing of bullets. "You stay here with Isaac," he shouted and took off. I hid in the bushes with Isaac, counting the seconds he was gone. Time plays cruel tricks. When you want it to slow down, it accelerates. If you need it to hurry, it laughs at you.

Finally the shooting stopped. Isaac huddled next to me behind the bushes in anxious compliance. For all I knew, the Nazis had won the skirmish. It wasn't until I saw Papa running down the hill that I shrieked with joy. Covered in soot, he scooped us in his arms.

The Nazis killed 11 forest residents. I didn't ask for their names. We climbed back up to the camp, where prayers cleansed the bodies of the dead. A cool wind shook the birch trees as I nestled against Papa's shoulder. "Will the Nazis attack us again? Is this the end?" Papa said nothing. We sat in tense silence with the others for a long time.

Suddenly my bare legs felt the rumble of tanks. Soon I could hear their mechanized sabers rolling closer. They are coming for us. This is it. "Don't let go of me, Papa," I begged. "Don't let go!" "Never," he said. "I'm here." The soldiers were singing a triumphant, vaguely familiar song. "Do you hear that, Papa? It's Russian!"

A line of tanks commanded by tough-looking Soviet men halted in front of us. "You are liberated, Jewish partisans," they announced. "The Germans are defeated. You can go home." Papa whirled me in the air, just like Mama did when I came home from *shul*. Mama was gone, yet they both held me now.

A soldier called to me in Russian. "Come up here little girl. The little boy too." He lifted us on the tank, laughing. Then he broke down. Either we were the sorriest, most bedraggled children he'd ever seen or we reminded him of his own. He wiped his eyes and handed me a half-empty bottle of *Somagonka*. "Have a drink, little princess!" Papa, who was standing beside the tank during the entire exchange, popped his head up, thanked the soldier and carried us away.

I danced with Papa, Isaac and our friends. We rejoiced. We cried. The men drank *Somagonka* and sang partisan songs. My father laid us on the straw in our tents and went outside again. He did not join Tuvia and his brothers, who discussed options for 1,200 unwanted Jews late into the night.

Papa consulted no one, not even us. He had made up his mind. I lay awake under the tent, which flapped in the breeze. I was afraid to stay, and afraid to leave.

The following morning, Tuvia addressed us for the last time. It was a beautiful, poignant speech. The Naliboki bore witness to our awe. He issued certificates verifying our participation in the unit so no one could accuse us of collaborating with the enemy.

His final blessing was freedom's heaviest burden — the right to choose the road ahead. Before we could start a new life, he said we had to destroy the old one. Tuvia ordered the partisans to blow up the camp. Papa helped set the charges.

After stuffing a few belongings in our knapsacks, I wandered down to the river where I had bathed only a day or so earlier. Isaac giggled at a squirrel. I did not share his care-free attitude.

I had cursed this forest for years. Now I would never see it again. Sadness tightened my chest. Just like the nuanced shades of snow and grass that I met in the Naliboki, I realized that emotions also had colors — red, white, purple, yellow, green, gray. I was growing up.

Thunderous orange and black explosions annihilated all traces of our existence. Isaac shook violently in the bushes and refused to budge until he saw his father. Papa's face was covered in powdery soot. "I have something to tell you," he announced. "The Jews are going back to Novogrudek to search for their families. We are never going back. This is final. I'm sure that many people there would love to kill us, even now."

"Where will we go?" I asked. "Who will want us?" "Lida," Papa said. "We're going to Lida. I heard there might be open-ings in a brewery there, and that would be a good opportu-nity for us."

Then he took me aside. "You should know that Chana is coming with us. Please be nice to her. I know she can never be your mother. But things will work out — at least I hope they will."

Then he rubbed my head and escorted us up the hill. My lungs choked on sulfur and smoke. Our camp was a cemetery of burning wood, utensils, singed clothing and melted cups.

Knapsack-laden Jews started forming an obedient line that would lead them in the direction of Novogrudek. I pitied them and envied them. I said goodbye to the group that shared our bunker during the typhus epidemic and searched for Lufka in the crowd. There were too many people. I never saw Lufka again, except in my heart.

Tuvia Bielski strode through the debris and hugged my father with his powerful arms. Drops of rain began falling like tears. "Goodbye, my dear friend," he said. "Take care of these darling children." "I will," Papa smiled. Together for three years, they had committed every detail to memory — including how Tuvia aimed his gun at Isaac. They never spoke of that. The rain had washed them clean. All I felt was their indissoluble bond.

I tugged at Tuvia's sleeve. "Goodbye, Commander," I said. He bent low and touched his lips to my outstretched hand.

"Farewell, Miss Koladicki. I know we will meet again." As usual, he was right.

After a horse-and-carriage ride, we boarded the train for the 30-mile trip to Lida, a Russian town slightly larger than Novogrudek. Too excited to sleep, I stuck my head out the window and let the hot wind tangle my hair. Something wonderful accompanied us in that dilapidated train. It was the future, and I was ready.

We found a place in Lida almost immediately — a tiny, isolated shack with a kitchen, storage closet and a fairly large room. There was an outhouse and a boney cow in the backyard. Chana divided the largest space into bedrooms by hanging a curtain down the middle. She and Papa took one side, and Isaac and I slept on the other side.

Then Papa told me he was going to the brewery to apply for the buyer's position and invited me to join him. The ability to go anywhere I desired just because I felt like it hit me like a revelation.

On the way, Papa stopped at a Russian school. "Tomorrow I'll enroll you here, so dust off your brains," he warned. I'd never been to school, and my heart spun like a top. I wasn't afraid. I was excited. And I never confused the two emotions again.

Papa got the job and bought me some candy at the grocery store. Chana was so pleased for my father that she cooked a celebratory dinner of cabbage and potatoes. I took my seat at the rickety table and lunged at my first real meal in three years.

I turned to say something to Isaac but he was fast asleep in his chair. As Lida's street lamps flickered and faded, I slipped into my own bed and babbled on and on about the day's adventures to Mama. I knew I was talking to myself, but deep inside I believed she could hear me.

TOP: My father Wolf Koladicki's family before the war. Papa, just 20, is second from the right. His younger brother Alec, on the far left, survived the Holocaust. Chana Gute Koladicki, Papa's mother, is next to Alec. Papa's three sisters Feitche, Chaike and Basha, also seen here, perished in the Holocaust.

RIGHT: My grandmother Chana Gute Koladicki next to her mother's grave in Novorgrudek, 1937. The Koladicki family had roots in the region for centuries. Chana Gute always wore a long black shawl when she visited the cemetery.

RIGHT: Wolf Koladicki at age 30, right around the time he married my mother Sarah. My brother Isaac found this rare photograph. We have no pictures of my mother.

BOTTOM: I am about to go on my first car ride to my first piano lesson in Forhenwald, the DP camp in Germany. I really loved the flute, but my father said a girl had no business playing a *fayfl* (whistle.)

RIGHT: Isaac and I prepare to go sledding in Forhenwald. Although we are growing up, I hold my brother with my hands. I always kept my arms around Isaac in the war.

LEFT: With Isaac at his wedding to Zahava in Chicago, 1963. Looking handsome and happy, he towers over me even in my heels — yet now and always, he remains my little brother.

RIGHT: My father Wolf at Isaac's wedding, 1963, two years before Papa suffered a massive stroke.

BOTTOM: Papa and I embrace at my son Steven's Bar Mitzvah in Denver, 1973. The stroke paralyzed my father on one side. He could no longer speak. But he refused to miss his grandson's passage into manhood in the Jewish faith. I call this photograph "My Hero."

Border Guards and Dancing Bears

Children's laughter untied the ribbon of sleep. I rolled over on my stomach, desperate to prolong the dream. Yet the bed felt so real! Then it all flooded back. I was no longer in the Naliboki. We left the forest days ago and moved into a shack in Lida. Instead of prowling through grass or bushes, I relieved myself in a private outhouse. Liberation dazzled me, up to a point. The past warned me to tread carefully. I walked on solid, civilized streets that covered quicksand, putting one foot in front of the other.

True to his word, Papa enrolled me in the Russian school where the teachers allowed me to enter fifth grade. I could already speak and read the language. Learning was incredibly exciting. History, literature, poetry — they dangled like keys to an alternate universe.

Like all Russian students, I was forced to belong to the Young Pioneer Youth Organization. In the Naliboki, Jews feigned allegiance to the Soviet partisans. We had no choice. But in school I used my mind as a weapon. An unfriendly student found ways to taunt me. One day she forced me to recite the Socialist creed in Russian. Clutching my red Pioneer kerchief, I performed effortlessly. That girl never bothered me again.

I walked through an open market to and from school. If I had enough pocket money, I bought candy. When I had time, I went an hour out of my way to visit a photographer's studio. The owner, a subdued, kind man who never asked questions, gladly accepted my curiosity. I stared at photographs of families and street scenes, juxtaposing my private loss and turmoil with these unremarkable images. The mundane is an exquisite balm for the tempest-tossed soul.

I was so engaged in the world that I was unaware of new life growing inside Chana's body. For all those months, Papa didn't speak of it either. A few days after Chana gave birth, the newborn died. My father and Chana brought the baby to the cemetery for a proper Jewish burial.

Chana attributed her misfortune to one of her innumerable superstitions. "Lida is bad luck for us," she told Papa. "I must leave here." Although he did not share her antiquated belief system, Papa obliged. We packed our satchels and left, liberated Jews on the road to nowhere in particular.

The Germans surrendered to the Allied Forces on May 7, 1945. Jews were left to wander like defeated, anonymous ghosts in this new Europe. The Nazis destroyed our papers when they forced us into the ghetto in 1941. When we escaped to the forest, the Koladicki family disappeared. Liberation enabled us to rejoin the human race but our identities had been obliterated.

Now that countries had regained their independence, they established rigorous border regulations. Jews were not alone on this paperless journey. Homeless voyagers found themselves ensnared in bureaucracy. Once you crossed a country's border you were safe — but getting there was a nightmare. We crossed at night, scurrying under barbed wire fences like rats. When we reached the other side, guards sprayed us with cans of DDT to disinfect us.

Our first stop after Lida was Lodz, the third largest city in Poland. According to the 1931 census, 202,487 Jews lived within the medieval parameters of the old quarter. When the Nazis took control in 1939, more than 200,000 Polish Jews were interred in the infamous Lodz Ghetto. In 1944, the ghetto was liquidated. Only 900 Jews survived.

I vaguely remember seeing the ghetto, a desolate crater of destruction that people passed on their way to somewhere else. Papa located a rundown, adequate apartment around a huge courtyard. I attended a Yiddish-speaking school with other Jewish children who survived the Holocaust. I've always wondered why we never talked about our mutual suffering. After three or four months, Papa decided it was time to move on.

The bombs had spared Waldenburg, a beautiful town with a quaint restaurant that served pickle soup. Oh, how I loved that soup. I attended a Catholic school, where a priest conveyed rigid dogma in a long black robe crowned by a starched white collar.

Every morning, the students intoned Latin prayers to a God whose death they blamed on the Jews. I stood with them, uncomfortable yet unwilling to reveal my heritage. Finally I told the priest that I was Jewish and could not say those prayers. I used the derogatory term *Zedouova*, the word Poles used for Jewess. The priest was visibly upset. "Do not use that word again," he instructed me. "It's bad."

Then he said I could stand up during prayers but no longer

had to recite them. His unexpected kindness surprised me like flowers blooming in winter.

One day Papa told us we were going to the American Zone in Germany. I hid my anxiety. While I trusted him implicitly, the idea of living in the country that tried so hard to kill me tied me in knots.

Yes, the Germans had lost the war — but they succeeded in murdering six million Jews, including my mother. Hatred does not shed its skin like a snake. It lies in wait for the next chance to attack. "The Americans will protect us," Papa calmed me. "You'll see."

In the meantime, I had to cross another border. Papa got us on a train bound for Germany carrying Greek Jews from Solinika. Jews may all believe in one God but they are as vast and individuated as the stars. We did not understand each other's language, only our scorched heritage.

I had no papers. Papa told me to keep quiet, but if an official confronted me I should say, "Soloniki." "They will think you are just another Greek Jew and let you alone," he advised. So when the overweight man with the greasy cap pulled me aside, I demurely offered, "Soloniki." It worked.

The train stopped in an abandoned area. Following Papa's inner compass, we walked and walked until a long barbed wire fence barred our way. I held Isaac's hand and pushed him underneath the fence.

"Ignore the barking dogs," I whispered. "They don't like the taste of children." Papa and Chana brought up the rear. When we reached the other side, a sign proclaimed a wondrous new word: Czechoslovakia.

The guards deloused us with DDT and then we were off to Prague. The very name evoked Jewish myth and majesty. When I was six, Papa mesmerized me with the story of the Golem. Rabbi Judah Loew ben Bezalel, the Maharal of Prague, resurrected the Golem to protect the Jews against their enemies in the Middle Ages.

As my feet touched the ancient cobblestones of Prague, the legend of the Golem accompanied me. No one could hurt me now. Papa intuited my excitement. "Children, let's go to the circus," he announced. "I think it's time to have some fun." My father adored the circus, especially the animals.

Inside the thick canvas tent, curious organ music ran sinister fingers down my spine. Animal smells filled my nose.

Eager children leaned over on the hard benches, mesmerized by clowns and prancing horses. Isaac stomped his feet with the crowd, and I dissolved in laughter. After those terrible years in the ghetto and forest, I was a normal child enjoying a normal day. It was extraordinary.

Horseback riders wearing sparkling costumes paraded before us. Rouged women dangled from ropes. Huge brown bears danced and bowed to applause. I looked at Papa, anticipating a big smile. Instead, tears slid from his eyes.

Was he weeping for our lost childhoods or because we could still laugh? I hugged him. "Don't be sad, Papa. We're at the circus!" "Yes, Paula," he brightened. "We are here."

Forhenwald

One year and nine months had passed since Russian tanks rambled into the Naliboki and set us free. I learned to adapt to the ambience of each new town. I acquired languages like other children collect marbles. And sometimes, as I watched snowflakes circling the lamplights or read a book on a park bench, I almost felt ordinary. Then a nightmare would yank off my arrogant cover. Poor Papa must have slept with one foot on the floor every night, expecting me to cry out.

I arrived at the Displaced Persons (DP) camp at Forhenwald, located in the American Zone near Munich, in 1946. I was 11 years old. The Germans we encountered on the way to the camp were exceptionally docile, almost afraid, and their fear emboldened my courage.

American MPs proliferated like trees in Forhenwald. They were muscular, tough, and walked around in a perpetual haze of cigarette smoke. Whether the MPs acknowledged me with a snappy "Hey, kid" or a respectful salute, I knew no one could hurt me in this place.

We lived with my father's cousin and his wife in an upstairs apartment in a former Nazi youth building that had indoor plumbing. A curtain separated the private areas. One of the first things my father did was nail a large mirror to the wall. Tired of constantly hearing that I was very pretty, I ignored the compliment and had erased the adjective from my mind a long time ago.

However, I admit I was curious. I secretly approached the large mirror when I was alone. I parted my hair in straight lines and carefully wound neat braids. The mirror was still a utilitarian object rather than a receptacle for vanity. That would change over time.

Several Bielski partisans and their families lived at Forhenwald. If they spoke about the war, they made sure I was not privy to their conversations. And that was fine. I paid attention to my own needs and desires. Life was good.

School was glorious because all my friends were Jewish. I became quite popular. Girls always pulled me aside to confide their problems. Apparently I offered wise counsel. The old soul I carried since early childhood had survived intact.

One day in 1947 I came home early from school. Whisky and half-eaten snacks littered the apartment. Men laughed, weaved unsteadily and patted my father on the back. Papa said nothing when I entered the room. Chana averted her gaze. No explanation was necessary, or forthcoming.

After living together as man and wife for six or seven years, Papa and Chana finally made it official. This was their wedding reception. I wish I could say the wedding weakened the rivalry between me and Chana, but it only intensified her possessiveness. A few months later, my half sister Fay was born. I loved her the second I held her.

Residents in the DP camp were forbidden to buy, sell, or engage in any form of commerce. The majority of us kept kosher, restricting ourselves to food prepared under rabbinical supervision that conformed to Jewish law. We had learned to do without during the war, but now people started clamoring for kosher meat, especially around the Jewish holidays. My father gathered some of his friends together and proposed a solution.

The men pooled their money and asked some German farmers living adjacent to the forest outside Forhenwald whether they would sell them some cows. Desperate for cash, the Germans quickly agreed. The farmers delivered the cows to the woods in back of the camp at night to avoid the MP on duty.

Papa and his friends unloaded the animals from the truck and escorted them to our resident *schochet*, or ritual slaughterer. He performed his duties admirably. Everyone was happy. The Jews had kosher meat and the German farmers had extra cash.

Another delivery was scheduled before Passover. Papa got wind that the MPs were planning to intercept the shipment, but there was another problem. A spring snow covered the ground, making normally invisible animal tracks as clear as a signed confession. Not to be outsmarted, Papa assembled his partners. "Don't worry," he told them. "I have devised a scheme. Each one of you must bring two pairs of boots to the farmers' truck."

After unloading the cows, Papa instructed his partners to "turn the boots *backward* so the heels are in front. Put the cows' hooves inside the boots and tie them securely with a rope." The men took the cattle to the *schochet* and sold the meat.

A few hours later, MPs screeched into camp on their jeeps

and searched the grounds. There were no cows, alive or dead. The MPs carefully scoured the heavy snow for animal tracks. Nothing.

All they discovered were male boot prints heading out of Forhenwald toward the forest. Empty handed but mad as hell, the soldiers arrested my father and took him to the police station. After five days, they released him for lack of evidence.

Zionism was encouraged among the Jewish youth in Forhenwald. Although I had never paid much attention to Palestine, I soon evolved into a passionate Zionist.

I joined Betar, the revisionist, hardline Zionist youth movement founded by Ze'ev Jabotinsky. Several of my friends opted for Hashomer-Hatzair, which was too leftist for my taste. When Israel won statehood in 1948, I was chosen to carry her new blue and white flag at the school assembly. I was so proud.

A representative of Histadrut, Israel's labor union, came to our school one day. She talked to all of us about moving to Israel and helping this new and astounding nation of Jews. Afterward she scanned the room and approached me. "Paula, your teacher says you are very bright. She also says you love Israel." "Yes, very much." "Would you like to live there?" I gasped. "Absolutely!"

For years I narrowly evaded an irrational, undeserved death warrant. Now I was willing to pay the ultimate sacrifice for Israel. That afternoon I told Papa that I wanted to go to Israel and fight for my people. "No, Paula, I won't allow it. This is not the right time," he said tersely. Arguing was useless. I knew when I was beaten.

One sumptuous spring morning, my life took another turn. A boy I often spoke to about art paused at my desk. He was the same boy. I was the same girl. Yet something suddenly changed. I felt inexplicably light-headed and happy.

I came of age in the forest, without a mother or books to prepare me for this moment. I made friends with his sister so I had an excuse to visit his house. For a month, we were inseparable. Then I tired of the relationship and my interest gravitated toward other boys. There are no guidelines for adolescent love. But I will always cherish that first blush of infatuation.

In the Naliboki, Papa loved to entertain us with stories of

South Africa, where his two brothers lived. "Wouldn't that make a good home for us when the madness ends?" he would smile.

In 1948, however, South Africa was ruled by the pro-Apartheid Afrikaner-dominated National Party and *Broederbond* organizations. In Forhenwald, we finally obtained papers to join my uncles. Papa threw them in the trash. "I saved you from one fascist regime," he said, "and I'm not taking you to another one."

My father then applied to go to America, which had enacted a strict quota system for Jewish refugees. The U.S. felt sorry for the Jews but did not seem to want us in her midst. We remained displaced persons for more than four years.

Finally the American Consulate in Munich mailed us a letter telling us we could apply for U.S. visas. That's when Papa told me his terrible secret. Ever since his arrest in Forhenwald over the cattle, he knew that any record of the incident would destroy his chances of entering the U.S. All our hopes hinged on one report.

On the appointed day we took the streetcar to the American Consulate in Munich. I wore my maroon coat with the leopard collar. Isaac tugged at his little cap a hundred times, and little Fay slumbered beneath her crocheted blanket. Papa and Chana struggled for composure.

Once inside the embassy, a soldier directed us to the visa department where a gray-haired man inspected us officiously. "Is this everything?" he asked after collecting our papers. "It's all there," Papa attested. "OK," the man said, "I'll be back in a minute. I just have to check a few things."

Time stopped. Papa and I exchanged nervous glances. The man returned, ran his fingers through his slick hair and cleared his throat. "You're good to go," he said in American slang. "Best of luck in America!"

I thought of Mama, her sisters Rivka, Chana and Grunya and her brother Shepa, and Papa's sisters Feitche, Chaike and Basha. Hidden under the earth, they would not be joining us.

Forhenwald, which means "pine forest" in German, had been my sweet-scented companion. The supreme irony is that Germany, the birthplace of Nazism, breathed new life into my crippled Jewish soul. My pine forest imparted many gifts: a proud identity, my first infatuation, a baby sister, disappearing cows, a maroon coat, an American visa, and a passionate love of Israel.

When I traveled to the Jewish state for the first time in 1972, I got off the plane, kissed the ground and cried. Six million tears mixed with mine.

Skyscrapers, Coke Machines and Hot Dogs

We boarded the New York-bound plane to America on a foggy Munich morning in 1949. I was 14. As I mounted the narrow stairway to the unknown, I did not look behind me. A starch-suited stewardess greeted me at the entrance to the airplane. Papa seemed relieved. Chana became ill before we even left the runway. I sat next to Isaac, eight years old and ecstatic, and held little Fay on my lap. The stewardess performed a head count — two, four, fifteen, twenty, thirty. "Put on your seat belts," she instructed.

Planes weren't pressurized then, and many people got sick as the cabin lurched and lifted. A powerful force nailed me to my seat. The plane rose higher, cut through the clouds and gradually leveled off in unbroken blue skies. Papa leaned across the narrow aisle and asked if I was all right. No words were necessary. The excitement in my gut could have powered our entire journey.

There are no signs or markers in the ocean, only endless, cyclical waves. I let my mind race ahead to the new world awaiting us. The only sound that distracted me was Chana's vomiting. The bubbling bromide the stewardess gave her was useless. Chana improved when we landed in Newfoundland for refueling. We ate in a fancy restaurant with tablecloths and fine silverware. The food was exceptional.

After a two-hour layover, we embarked on the last leg of our journey. The ghetto and the Naliboki receded in time and distance. "Look!" the passengers began murmuring, "New York City!" I was incredulous. "There's the Statue of Liberty, Papa! And the Empire State Building is right over there!" The plane circled and descended. Her wheels skidded on the landing strip and roared to a stop. Eternity had evaporated in the blink of an eye.

We stayed in a dilapidated hotel off Broadway. Human bodies and traffic competed in the streets. From elegant ladies in high heels to poor unkempt men, everyone converged on New York City. In this bastion of noise and speed, Novogrudek seemed like an archaic fantasy. If I didn't focus on something specific, I might get lost in a million tantalizing directions.

The hotel's Coke machine proved a worthy adversary. I

examined that contraption for hours, determined to unlock its secrets. After a few entreaties, my pockets bulged with Papa's spare change. I put a silver nickel in the slot and a cup dropped. Coke syrup poured from one spigot while bubbly water cascaded from another. Uniting in the cup, a baffling alchemy transpired. Coke! This world was full of sweet surprises.

Five days later we took the train from New York to Chicago, where my father had relatives. The Joint Distribution Committee helped us find an apartment in the Jewish neighborhood on Chicago's west side. Rent control was still in effect, which meant Papa had to buy the previous tenants' furniture.

The stove looked like it was from the 1880s and the chipped kitchen table hobbled back and forth during mealtime. But the rent was only $47 a month. A neighbor in our building fed me hot dogs every Sunday. Nothing tasted better than her hot dogs — steaming hot, juicy and brimming with sauerkraut and mustard.

Papa found a job carrying heavy vats of meat at a sausage company. One day, a worker who didn't like my father's accent insulted him in front of all the workers. Papa picked up a vat of sausage, poured it over the man's head and walked out. My father didn't understand English very well, but he had no trouble translating verbal abuse.

He later opened a successful butcher shop. Waking up at 5 a.m., he personally went to the best market to select the finest cuts of meat. Chana helped out in the shop, where Fay napped peacefully in her buggy.

Papa's Chicago family — three aunts and several cousins — defined our social galaxy. Warm and welcoming, they included us in every wedding and joyous occasion. I was fortunate. Too many survivors emerged from the horror without parents, spouses or children. I had my father, my brother and a profusion of relatives.

The war had ended five years ago. Our relatives wanted to ask Papa so many questions. They had read the news reports in the paper and seen the ghastly photographs. "Did the Nazis really lock Jews in showers and burn them in ovens?" "How did you survive with two children in a forest?"

Trusting their instincts, they kept silent until Papa opened the floodgates of memory in my absence. I know because I overheard several subdued conversations when I was in my bedroom or washing dishes in the kitchen.

It was as if the Holocaust belonged to adults only. Perhaps my relatives couldn't bear the thought of children drowning in that quicksand, or wanted to believe that I'd forgotten everything. They never once said Mama's name.

Although I passed the high school entrance exam, I enrolled in the eighth grade at William Penn Elementary one block away from our apartment. I wanted to perfect my grammar.

Every day my senses bounced like poodle skirts down the hallways. There was so much to learn! Introduced to Spin the Bottle at a party, I preferred Fred Astaire's flirtatious, graceful partnering of Ginger Rogers on the big screen.

An adept chameleon, I learned how to blend in with my contemporaries so expertly that the class voted me the girl most likely to succeed. I bought a white taffeta dress downtown to wear at the graduation dance. My friends never brought up my origins or thick Yiddish accent. Like the majority of American Jews, they suspected but left it alone.

High school loomed like a fork in the road. I could

continue my education in a noisy, assimilated school or choose a Jewish institution. I did not hesitate. I wanted to study with other Jewish students. The Chicago Jewish Academy was very prestigious — and expensive. One summer morning I walked two blocks to Crawford Avenue and waited for the red and beige Chicago streetcar to pull up. Feeling slightly weak in the knees, I paid the driver my student fare and rode to the academy.

Brandishing my transcripts from William Penn, I interrupted the secretaries and demanded to see Dr. Babad, the principal. "Do you have an appointment?" "No." "Why to you want to see Dr. Babad?" "Because I want to go to school at the Chicago Jewish Academy." "Are your parents with you?" "No, but that is irrelevant. This is my idea. And I won't leave until I see him."

The woman closest to Dr. Babad's closed office buzzed the principal and whispered into the receiver. The half-audible exchange lasted one agonizing minute. Finally the woman ushered me inside. I explained to this austere and gentle man that I had a father, a stepmother, and no money. We spoke for about 15 minutes. Then he shook my hand and said I could start school in September.

Life at home became increasingly volatile. Emotional wounds inflicted in the Holocaust gradually bled into the marriage. Animosity replaced affection. Chana would hurl Yiddish curses at my father: "May you never live to walk your kids down the aisle at their wedding."

In 1950, Chana underwent gallbladder surgery and stayed in the hospital for five days. Robbed of a mother's love at such an early age, Isaac had transferred his affection to Chana years ago.

I will never forget how Isaac jumped up and down when she came home from the hospital. He ran to her with outstretched arms. Chana ignored him and rushed straight over to Fay. Isaac waited as long as hope allowed, then quietly slipped into another room. It broke my heart. Despite all the love in his life now, there will always be a hole inside him.

Love, Children, and the Commander

All 17-year-olds are vulnerable to love, that irresistible stirring in the blood. I wasn't immune, but for some reason I never felt compelled to have a boyfriend. Instead of going steady, I spent every available moment with David and Jerry, my closest friends. We met by accident at the corner soda shop. Something about Jerry seemed familiar. Then I remembered we were at the same summer camp for teenage Jewish survivors in Germany.

The three of us were inseparable. I wore my gold and white saddle shoes to the soda shop, the movies, on car rides and evening walks —wherever innocence took us. This friendship satisfied all my needs, but not theirs.

One day they told me that they both loved me in that "special" way and gave me an ultimatum: "You have to pick one of us." I stared at them. "Can I at least think about this?" They considered my request. "You have one day, starting right now." I chose David. And there was no going back.

David survived the Holocaust with his family in Siberia.

Almost two years older, he was charismatic, confident, and exuded undeniable magnetism. I felt like I'd known him forever. It's as if we were bound together. This collision of romantic attraction is a very common occurrence — but for us it was unlike anything else in the world.

Papa recognized that David and I were falling in love, but he thought that we were too young to survive the inevitable storm. One day he put his foot down and refused to let David and me see each other again. Was my father unaware that nothing fans the flames of young love higher that opposition? David and I found ways to talk to each other through open windows on spring nights. Sometimes we met secretly for a few moments.

Hoping to diffuse my feelings for David, Papa gave me permission to date my best friend Jerry. I was going to say no until David devised a very clever scheme. David would drive to our apartment with a lovely girl sitting next to him in the front seat. Jerry came to the door, made small talk with Papa, escorted me to the car and helped me inside the back seat. Once we were safely out of sight, I moved up front with David while his "date" slipped in the back seat with Jerry.

This pretense continued until I finally found the courage to tell my father that David and I were getting married. Papa cried. He defeated the Nazis but could not impede the course of young love. "David is only 18," he challenged me. "What are you going to live on?" He knew his arguments were pointless.

Papa threw up his hands. "Go ahead," he said, "do what you want." David and I were married on November 25, 1951. My father's opposition melted and he accepted his son-in-law with open arms. David's parents welcomed me into their family. We didn't have any money. We had each other. That was enough.

Susan, my first child, was born in 1952. I had no mother to instruct me on parenting or even challenge my ideas. I really missed Mama during my first pregnancy. Like most expectant mothers in the 1950s, I bought Dr. Spock's book on childrearing. After reading about 25 pages at the blue table in our kitchen, I had enough. "This is stupid," I said, discarding the book.

According to Dr. Spock, mothers should adhere to a strict feeding schedule. I could only feed my baby every four hours

117

regardless of hunger. There also was a section about letting your baby cry. I'm a very logical person. Why would a baby cry unless it needs something? So I made up my own rules, and they worked. Freda was born 14 months after Susan, and Steven completed the circle in 1960.

I have always been afraid of lightning and thunder, but I never allowed my kids to see my fear. I did not want them to inherit my anxiety. You don't compromise your children's happiness with your own monsters. As my children grew up, I tried to keep my childhood on the other side of the ocean.

Much later, I asked my kids for their impressions of me as a new mother. They said I was never scared, always brave and a lot of fun. Susan and Freda still laugh about the carrot soup. Once I served them some carrot soup I slaved over for hours. It did not meet with their approval. They despised that soup! If that's the worst sin I committed, I'm pretty confident that I succeeded as a parent.

I integrated all my experiences and attributes — the pre-war tomboy, the scared girl in the forest, the modern American mother — into one personality. The old traumas periodically resurfaced. The past devoured the present. I still have nightmares. Yet my children always pulled me back. I gave them life, but in ways too numerous to count, they saved mine.

There was Susan's first word, Freda's first step, Steven's first uneven gallop across the carpet. Every time I witnessed their achievements, I instinctively looked for my mother. If only Mama could participate in my happiness! I missed her so during those simple, phenomenal moments.

One autumn afternoon, as leaves skipped across the cracked Chicago pavement, I dropped by my father's apartment. "Paula, there's someone here who wants to says hello." A tall man stood up from the couch. It was Tuvia Bielski. I froze in disbelief, and he searched for traces of the little girl in the young mother. "Paula," he bowed, repeating that long ago gesture from our first meeting in the Naliboki. "Commander," I whispered, extending my hand.

"Have a drink with us," suggested Papa, who gently nudged Tuvia's side. "My Paula is married and a mother. Can you believe it?" Tuvia tugged at his suit self-consciously. "The years have forced me to accept many things I once thought impossible," he acknowledged. "Sit next to me, Paula. I'm starting a business back East and I've been trying to convince Wolf to join me. He has declined my offer."

I listened as Papa and Tuvia returned to the Naliboki in that unexceptional Chicago apartment. The contrast between past and present was jarring. I wanted to stay close to this humbled, godlike man for hours, but adult responsibilities beckoned.

After a few sips of vodka and some pieces of herring, I explained that I had to run to the market and then pick up my kids. I excused myself hurriedly, without ceremony or significance. I remember looking at Tuvia and saying, "Thank you for saving my life." I'm not even sure he heard me.

I have little tolerance for regret. It's a useless emotion. But I will always regret the things I did not say to Tuvia that fall afternoon. I never saw him again.

Tuvia Bielski died in 1987 in Brooklyn. While he had difficulty finding his place after the war, he loved his adoring wife and children who cherished and sustained him. Tuvia was fond of saying, "I'll be famous after I'm dead." As usual, he was correct.

Writers, historians and Hollywood rediscovered Tuvia

Bielski in the 1990s and over the next decade. The Jewish partisans have never forgotten him. Their stories, and mine, are inextricably linked to his. Each October we gather in New York to celebrate the man and honor his heroism. Our numbers dwindle every year. There aren't many of us left. But as long as we live, we will remember our commander.

During the Holocaust we could not see beyond the next hill, let alone mountains of time. As the years passed, we climbed those mountains. Now my children's children are young adults. Isaac earned an accounting degree, sang in synagogues and married Zahava on a hot August day in 1963. Their children have blessed them with many grandchildren.

David and I were married for 26 years. We built a family, a business and many wonderful memories together. But it was not to be. After struggling to overcome the problems that arose in the relationship, we divorced in 1978.

Papa's Last Premonition

Papa's life was not extraordinary, but it was satisfying. He toiled in his butcher shop, watched "Flash Gordon" or "The Lone Ranger" on TV and tenderly embraced his grandchildren. Still, the smile that stiffened my courage in the Naliboki diminished in frequency.

He was no longer playful. I can see him sitting in his favorite chair, his eyes drifting across time and space to the Holocaust — and my mother. He still felt responsible for her death. I knew that Mama never doubted him, or his love. I wanted to tell him this, but his grief was a private place I dared not disturb.

One day in 1965, Papa stopped at my house after work. As we sat at the kitchen table, I sensed that he wanted to say something but couldn't find the words. Suddenly he started crying. "Paula," he quivered, "I have a terrible feeling that I'm going to die."

Fear cut my vocal chords. When I found my voice, it was indignant. "Of course you're not going to die!" I said, trying to calm him down. I also had to calm myself, because I believed him. Throughout the war, his uncanny ability to predict the future never faltered.

Despite my protestations, Papa couldn't stop sobbing. Finally he wiped his eyes, composed himself and walked to the front door. "You're not going to die!" I repeated. "I won't let you!" That night I was too troubled to eat or sleep.

Six months later, while cutting meat in the butcher shop, my father collapsed. Chana screamed for help, and the neighbors came running. The police rushed his inert body to the hospital. I followed with Chana and Isaac.

The doctors told us Papa had suffered a major stroke and was in a coma. Chana moaned incoherently. Isaac prayed. I whispered *Ikh hob dir lieb* — Yiddish for "I love you" — in his ear.

We hired a private nurse. One of us stayed at his bedside until she came on duty. One morning we walked in the room and discovered that Papa's arm was badly swollen. The night nurse had stuck his IV in the wrong spot, causing an infection. We fired her immediately. After that, we took shifts at the hospital. Chana took the morning shift, I stayed in the afternoon, and Isaac arrived after work.

On the 30th day of his coma, Papa regained consciousness. I was overjoyed until a battery of tests concluded that he would never talk or move the right side of his body again. Given my father's pride and temperament, the prognosis consigned him to a living hell. I searched his face for a sign. There was none, only rigid silence. Yes, he was alive — but it was not the life he fought for in the forest.

Once the hospital released Papa, I visited him every day. I lifted his heavy body in and out of the bathtub, loaded his wheelchair into his station wagon, took him to rehabilitation, waited for the hour to end and drove him home.

I spoke to Papa in Yiddish, telling him about my kids and avoiding subjects that might upset him. Hopelessness oozed from his skin. Occasionally his former self appeared in his eyes, but I felt his spirit was disappearing.

Papa was not a compliant patient. He would refuse to take his medicine. Chana would call and ask me to come over to the house. I'd sit on the bed, comforting him in Yiddish as I held the pills. "Please Papa, you must take them," I begged. "I can't lose you. Do it for me."

Finally he swallowed them. Then he would raise his useless

arm with his good hand and let it drop on his lap like stone. I interpreted that gesture as a wail: "How long do I have to live like this!"

Papa's speech was incoherent. His frustration only made things worse. Yet somehow, for reasons I'll never understand, he could sing with Isaac. Whenever Isaac practiced Jewish liturgical music, my father sang with him, his voice and pronunciation reaching the heavens in perfect clarity. Once the song ended, my father was mute again. The doctors could not explain this mysterious ability.

David and I decided to relocate our family to Denver in 1967 to take advantage of new opportunities. It was a necessary move that exacted a horrible price. I would have to leave Papa, my vulnerable dark star, in Chicago. I knew he was in gentle hands. Chana, in spite of their strained relationship, was a loving caretaker. Isaac was a deeply devoted son. But I have always imagined that Papa loved me more than anyone. He was my heart, and I always believed I was his.

One afternoon I sat on my father's bed and told him that moving to Denver offered us a new start. I had to take the chance. He wept so hard that tears drenched his paralyzed

Papa's Last Premonition

arm. Then he shook his head, lifted his good arm and waved at me. The gesture — "It's all right, now go!" — was both a farewell and blessing. It also was heartbreaking.

Three times a year, every year, I flew to Chicago to visit him. I provided animated progress reports on Susan, Freda and Steve. My tactful omissions of David during these one-sided conversations, which Chana interrupted with tea and fussing, required no elucidation. Our new start had failed. The marriage was over. But the children thrived in Denver, and I adored the mountains. I also began studying art seriously.

As I sat with my father on those affectionate visits — he was so happy to see me! — I often watched him sleep. His furrowed brow rarely relaxed, even as he dreamed. I stroked his head, timed my breathing to match his and murmured Yiddish endearments. Our goodbyes were choreographed dances of sweet kisses and willpower. "I'll see you soon," I'd smile cheerfully. The second I closed the front door, I doubled over in grief.

Despite the physical difficulties, my father came to Denver in the summer of 1973 for Stevie's Bar Mitzvah. I can see

127

Papa in his dark blue suit, a red yarmulke covering his head. He was so proud of Stevie, and Stevie was so proud of his grandfather. In November, 1973, Isaac accepted a position with the IRS and moved to Denver with his family. The liftoffs and landings that brought us to our father increased, and we were grateful for every one.

Papa had always hated the Jewish month of Shevat, which coincides with January-February on the Gregorian calendar. "Shevat is not a brotherly month," he used to say in that unmistakable mixture of Yiddish and Russian. On February 5, 1975 — 10 years after a stroke stole his speech and paralyzed half his body — my father died. Isaac was by his side.

The second the phone rang in Denver, my stomach fell. Papa's premonitions died with him, but mine were on alert. I put the receiver to my ear. "It's Isaac," my brother said. "He's gone." I telephoned the airline and managed to get on the next flight out of Denver. Then I called my children and David, who insisted he was coming with me to Chicago.

The plane landed, we caught a cab and went straight to the mortuary. Chana, who was rocking in a corner chair, didn't really notice me. Isaac rushed up and hugged me. Then he showed where they had laid Papa's body.

I asked the director to open my father's casket. The first thing I noticed was his *tallis*, which Isaac had draped around Papa's shoulders. I bent down, patted his cheeks and hands and kissed his cold cheek goodbye. My father, my hero, was at peace.

After the funeral, we decided that I would take Papa's body to Denver for burial. I don't remember if anyone objected, nor did I care. He never left me behind in life, and I was not going to leave him behind now.

We buried him at Mt. Nebo Cemetery, near the front gates. Isaac chose the inscription for the headstone: "Our souls are bound to his." When Chana passed away in 1995, we buried her next to my father.

I have stood before too many open graves in this cemetery. It is considered a Jewish *mitzvah*, or commandment, to shovel dirt into the hole at our feet. I can't bring myself to do this. The truth is I rarely visit Papa in this place. Where is he? I don't know — perhaps in the snow, a recollected smile, this story and the air I breathe.

Art is My Soul

For as long as I can remember, and wherever the Holocaust has taken me, colors riveted my attention. The artistic urge has many sources: memory, observation, imagination and impulse. I first touched the subtlety of color — gradating shades of snow, sky and grass —in the Naliboki. During quieter moments, when I wasn't fleeing from one place to the next, nature revealed its delicate palette.

I did not have the means to express these lessons until Forhenwald, when my botany teacher reprimanded me and made me stand in the corner. While I cared nothing for botany, I loved the fascinating beauty of leaves.

I stared at the wall until it sucked me inside. By the end of class, I had drawn leaves with light green chalk all over the wall. The teacher was angry. I was happy. This was my first artistic statement.

If we pay attention, life will offer us second chances. Not long after my divorce I met Sam. Although we didn't know each other, an easy reciprocity permeated our relationship. Being with Sam was like emerging from a hailstorm and being washed by gentle warm rain. We married in 1981. Our secure and loving relationship freed me to pursue my art.

My dream of becoming a painter sprang to life during a golf game, when I mentioned this passion to my golf partner. She was married to painter Mort Schneider. She invited me to their home after our game to meet him. Mort was in his studio. Cordial yet cool, he had one foot in the real world and one hand in the painting. I understood.

I asked Mort whether he ever accepted students. "Some-times," he said cryptically. He set me up by the window in his studio and asked me to draw something. I declined. He asked again. This time I drew a chair. He took me on as a student.

At our next lesson, Mort showed me a black and white photograph and told me to copy it. I painted large white flowers on a red background. I was so nervous that I just wanted to finish the assignment. "Where did you see these flowers?" Mort asked, confused. I circled the flowers with my index finger. "They're right there! Can't you see them?" His eyes grew large. "Now I can," he said. He signed my name: a capital P with a dot, and Burger in large letters.

I brought that first meager attempt home and set it on the

floor of the apartment. When Sam came home — he had collected art long before he collected me — he studied the painting for a few minutes. "Who did this?" he asked. "Me." "No kidding," he smiled. "You really are an artist!" It's not that I needed his approval. Still, his words fell like that warm rain I'd come to love so much.

When Mort first took me on, he saw a pupil eager to test the waters. He had no idea that I was a Holocaust survivor. I immediately explained my goals. I wasn't looking for therapy or a hobby or an escape from boredom. All I wanted to know was whether I had what it took to be an artist. One day he answered my question. "Yes, Paula, you have what it takes. But don't let it go to your head." I could breathe again!

Two years later, Mort declared that I was ready to leave him and advance to the next stage. Surprisingly, his statement upset me terribly. "What, are you trying to get rid of me?" I accused him. "No," he assured. "It's time for you to fly on your own wings."

At his suggestion, I enrolled at the Art Students League in Denver, where I had extraordinary teachers like Ramon Kelly and Dale Chisman. I devoted the next 10 years to studying and cultivating my art. Chisman told me once that many artists hesitate before a blank canvas, but I *attack* it. He was so right. I learned in the Holocaust that time is too ephemeral to waste.

The studio is my world. Art is my soul. Judging by the appearance of my studio, mine is a messy, unbounded soul that flits from abstracts to landscapes to flowers. Ideas constantly bounce in my head until my brain feels like a jar of marbles.

Nothing takes precedence over a newborn painting. I ignore the telephone, which is covered in oil and acrylic handprints. Even Sam stays away from this sacred space. Despite my age I stand on my feet for hours, freed from the aches and pains that would otherwise force me to stop. It's like running through the Naliboki on inexhaustible legs. Making it to the end is all that matters.

Everything in Judaism springs from light: Shabbat, holidays, memorial candles, menorahs. For me there is no greater symbol in Judaism than the *Chanukiah*, a menorah with nine candles. People are drawn to my Chanukah menorahs, and I love creating them. The winter holiday celebrates the Jewish people's survival over adversity, which is exactly what I witnessed in my childhood.

I don't have a map when I stand above the blank canvas. As I start painting a menorah, my hands move this way and that. Something speaks through me. I am both mesmerized recipient and conductor of the music.

After I outline the menorah, I choose random, vibrant colors for the arms and base. Frequently my choices reflect unconscious associations like the Sea of Eilat or Jerusalem's azure sky. I paint quickly, absorbed in my vision. I'm also aware of an organic, underlying intent. I change a line here and add another one there. Then I put the painting aside and walk away from it until the final pieces assemble in my mind.

I have occasionally ventured into the Holocaust in my artwork. Sometimes I create realistic images of actual events, and at other times I prefer a more abstract, stylized form. As Wordsworth wrote, some thoughts "often lie too deep for tears."

Art cast its spell on me when I was a frightened child. Now I'm all grown up, and then some. I adore my life, my husband, children, grandchildren and friends. But I want to be honest. Without art I'd feel dead; buried beneath an immense void.

Imagine a woman has a powerful passion inside her but she can't tell anyone. She's mute. Then finally, incredibly, she has a voice. It's like Papa singing with Isaac after the stroke destroyed his speech.

This is what art means to me. It helps me transcend the loss. I don't forget the shadows. They are always here. When I pick up a brush, I honor them — with light.

From the Mouths of Others

My brother Isaac, my children and grandchildren are not literary extensions of this Holocaust memoir. They interpret my experience in the context of their own lives. The Holocaust was my nightmare. Their narrative is the mirror. No memoir would be complete without their perspectives — so different from mine, and each other's.

Isaac was a little boy in the Holocaust. He did not comprehend the larger picture until much later. The innate limitations of childhood protected him from cruel realities: our mother's death, the odds against our survival, the Nazis' devotion to our annihilation.

Still, he knew what he knew. We are both much older now, but I will always be Isaac's big sister. And while we may never agree on everything, the love is secure.

Second-generation survivors Susan, Freda and Steven continue debating the Holocaust's effect on their mother. Sam's daughter Robbyn, whom I love as my own, has her own opinions.

Their insights — by turns amusing and chilling — paint the portrait of a woman who is unfazed, tenacious, funny, and trau-

matized. I can delineate their individual handprints and accept their veracity.

While I adore my nine grandchildren equally, I selected the three eldest to represent the third-generation survivors. Jessica, Alex and Sarah are very intelligent young adults blessed with a penetrating, challenging, creative intelligence.

Of course every grandmother says this about her grandchildren. Still, their introspection and analyses leave me breathless. If they are the light of the future, civilization will never again succumb to darkness.

I asked my co-writer Andrea Jacobs to interview my family. I did not wish to be present. What follows are not her words, nor mine.

The reflections of my brother, children and grandchildren, which come from their mouths alone, belong here — for the Holocaust claims not only the survivor but everyone she or he touches in its demanding wake.

Isaac

"Hello, hello," Isaac says. "Come inside. So what has Paula been telling you? I have a feeling you'd like some coffee. Am I right? Sit on the right side of the table while I make it. That way you can see my daughters' wedding pictures across the wall."

His daughters sparkle, for they are Isaac's jewels. His wife Zahava, who is in Baltimore, is the dark-haired diamond in the center. Papers scatter here and there. Isaac is not lonely, but the home feels a little empty.

"So," he says after setting the hot white cup on a holder, "Paula has told you about everything? I know many things too. I was just a little boy — not even three when it all started — but I remember details you wouldn't believe.

"Just so you know."

He's dressed for work. "My boss is gonna be saying a *mi shebeirach* (implying a reprimand) for me!" Isaac says sarcastically. "But I'll give you all the time you need. Do you know there's a blessing you say after drinking?" He recites it from a small prayer book.

Isaac, who has a magnetic personality, shares Paula's physical charm, the lilting accent, spontaneous humor and animated eyes.

Paula has portrayed Isaac as a small, carefree boy who didn't realize death was always knocking at the door. She constantly held his hand so he wouldn't be afraid or wander away.

Isaac no longer reaches for Paula's hand. A distinguished looking man in his early 70's, he is a glowing grandfather who wraps each grandchild in proud adjectives.

"How long have I known Paula?" Isaac strokes his gray beard ironically. "Well, I guess about as long as I can remember, because she remembers when I was born. But I can't vouch for that."

The first image he recalls is wading through a grassy field with Paula. "I don't know where we were. But my first memories of the Holocaust were in the Naliboki forest. It must have been October or November of 1942. We were running from one place to another. We didn't have a permanent home. The accommodations were bare. We slept under the bushes in little tents."

In every memory, Paula is there.

"She was kind of a skinny little girl, with braids," he recalls. "I was a bit chubbier. I liked to play outside. We had no Monopoly or TVs or cell phones. No anything.

"But there were all these animals outside — squirrels, foxes, rabbits.

"Obviously I looked up to Paula. We were like two little lambs in a herd. Next to my father, she was my big person to rely on. We lost our mother, so she was that motherly big sister for me.

"She kept an eye on me. When my father wasn't around, she was the authority. I looked to her for guidance. She was the Supreme Court!"

Protected in his innocence, Isaac was unaware of painful realities Paula comprehended all too well, particularly their mother's death. "No, I don't remember my mother," he says quietly.

Isaac remembers clashing with Paula after liberation, when he attended kindergarten in a church in Lida. "You know how they have rebbe cards now? Well, they had that concept 65 years ago. They were giving out cards of JC (Jesus Christ), Mary, Peter, Paul. It was the first time I ever saw colored cards.

"Paula took those cards away from me, which I didn't really appreciate. But she was bigger than me. Whatever explanation she gave me, I didn't understand. All I know is one minute I had the cards and the next minute they were gone."

Paula questioned everything from God's sanity to God's existence during the Holocaust. This has been difficult for Isaac, an observant Jew, to accept.

"There are a great deal of survivors who have problems about why God didn't intervene in the Holocaust," he says. "Our father had a different approach. He remained a faithful, traditional Jew."

Isaac traces the theological split between himself and Paula to his religious training in Chicago. "I went to a Jewish parochial school in Chicago, then Telshe Yeshiva and later Skokie Yeshiva. I also was a *schochet* (ritual slaughterer)."

He sketches the intersecting streets of the old Jewish neighborhood in Chicago on a large piece of paper. There were about five synagogues within walking distance, each one boasting a renowned cantor.

Isaac's vocal teachers transformed his innate musical aptitude into a superior talent that quickly attracted attention. By age 17 he no longer stood next to the cantor with the other boys. He stood by himself.

A respected cantor for more than 52 years, Isaac puts faith above doubt. "My father was a traditional Jew," he says. "He observed Shabbos. I learned how to *daven* from him. And I inherited his voice. He had a very nice voice."

Isaac pauses, as if he senses what's coming next.

"Of course I love Paula," he says. "I love all my relatives very much. But I am closer to Paula because we are bound by our experiences."

One hour turns into two hours. Isaac covers every inch of the Holocaust and the years that followed.

Isaac takes down several scrapbooks, pointing to his grandchildren with relish. "Look, see him with the fish?" "See how they all love their *Zaidy*?"

Late for work, he opens the front door and glances at the weather.

"Watch out for the rain," he says, standing in the hallway. Then he sighs.

"Paula was all I knew. She was all I knew."

Pieces of My Puzzle

"I don't remember my mother talking about the Holocaust while I was growing up," says Susan, a family law attorney and Paula's eldest child. "But I can't remember a time when *I didn't* know her story. I would sit with her as she looked out of her kitchen window, describing fragments of her life during the war."

The mother of two describes her childhood as idyllic. "I had fun all the time when I was a child. I still do. I never had to do the laundry or anything unpleasant. That was my mother's idea, because she never had a normal childhood.

"I can still see Mom getting dressed up to go out with my father on Saturday evenings in Chicago. She was so beautiful."

One Saturday night after her parents left, Susan wandered into the den. The babysitter was watching TV, which was airing a documentary about the Holocaust. "Somehow I realized my parents had been part of this," Susan says. "But my mom was an extremely appropriate parent.

"I assumed that she didn't have any personality problems

from the Holocaust because she was a child when it happened. But kids are extraordinarily perceptive. If you or I had witnessed that, we'd be traumatized."

After the 2008 release of the film "Defiance," the riveting cinematic portrayal of the Bielski partisans, Susan remembers helping her mother compose a speech about her experiences in the Naliboki.

"Here I am trying to get details and facts — but what she shared was how painful it was to lose her own mother. I don't think I fully realized what Mom went through until that moment. We never talked about this stuff, even to this day."

Paula constructed a protective bubble around Susan and her siblings. "It was a world where nothing bad could ever happen to us," she says, "and I understand why this was so important to her.

"The years have taught me that our lives are not so much about what happened to us as how we deal with it. We need to acknowledge those who came before us and suffered brutally.

"This is my mother's story. I regret that *she* will never forget."

• • •

Freda, Paula's second child, is a C.P.A. Married to Jerry, a cardiologist, she is the mother of five and never misses her kids' football games and school functions. In contrast to her older sister, Freda insists that her mother did not allow the Holocaust to define or dwarf her personality.

"She took what happened and moved forward," she says. "This is what's so unique about her.

"My mother is extremely focused, whether it's on the latest fashion trend or subtle political dynamics. You can't keep her stuck in the past regardless of the circumstances. She got through the Holocaust and went on with her life."

Freda recalls that all the adults who visited their Chicago home had vaguely familiar accents. "My parents' friends were all survivors," she realizes. Bonded by terrible secrets, they spoke in hushed tones to avoid being overheard by innocent ears.

Like Susan, Freda can't pinpoint the exact moment she learned about her mother's past, "but it seemed like I always knew. I guess she told us when she thought we were old enough to hear it.

"I learned I was the daughter of Holocaust survivors. They were my people. I never viewed this as a negative. I remember saying as a kid, 'I come from strong stock.'"

Years ago, when Paula asked Susan and Freda how she fared as a young mother, their opinion was unanimously positive — with the exception of some carrot soup she made for the kids.

"Oh that," Freda laughs. "What parent hasn't said to their child, 'You are going to sit at that table and eat X, Y or Z vegetable?' Every parent does that. What made this interesting was that neither Susan nor I wanted any part of that soup.

"I finally choked it down — and to this day I'd rather eat a shoe than a carrot. But Susan dug in her heels and refused. My sister would still be sitting at that table today."

Of all her mother's many lessons, Freda values the hard-won gift of self-reliance. "My mom taught us to trust our own instincts," she says. "This was the model fate chose for her as a child, and this is how she parented us.

"If you asked me how my mom would be different if she hadn't gone through the Holocaust, I wouldn't be able to answer because I don't see her as being defined by the Holocaust.

"She is the most forward-looking, big picture oriented person I know."

• • •

Steven, a lawyer, was born in 1960. Married to Alisa, an event planner, and the father of two grown children, he describes himself as "a man who cries easily. I'm easily moved, easily touched." Even this brief conversation dislodges his defenses.

"I really didn't understand the significance of my mother's history until I saw 'Defiance,'" says Steven. "I knew she was a survivor from a small town in Poland and that her mother had been murdered.

"But I didn't know anything about her time in the forest until she mentioned Nechama Tec's book *Defiance*, published in 1994. Eventually I began to ask her more questions, and she was more willing to talk about it."

A year ago, Paula finally spoke about the period in the forest that Steven says epitomizes his mother's Holocaust saga. "We were sitting at the table, and she told me that her stepmother Chana brought up a certain incident while being interviewed by Chana's granddaughter Jennifer," he recalls.

In the tape, Chana described Paula's immobilizing terror when Wolf did not return to the forest camp for weeks.

"My mother understood Polish and Russian, and she knew that she and Isaac would no longer be protected by the group. She grasped the incomprehensible. She would be killed. But she didn't want to die in a horrible way. She thought in her child's mind that if she remained perfectly still, death would find her.

"Although Mom always tells me how proud she is that she survived the Holocaust, she emphasizes that they were all resigned to dying in that forest."

When Steven was 22 or 23, he visited Yad Vashem, Israel's world-famous Holocaust museum. He has never recovered from that solemn, cathartic day.

"We were touring a library," he says. "There was a page for each person who died in the Holocaust. I could hear people typing in the background. It was 1982, and they were still trying to record all the names.

"I couldn't finish the tour. I went outside and sobbed. All

I knew was that whatever was in me, I didn't want to carry. I didn't want to be burdened by the pain I was feeling. It was too big for one person."

He describes Paula as "a queen. Not a diva . . . but you know you're not dealing with an ordinary woman. And being with her makes you stand taller."

Once Steven accompanied his mother to Greeley, where she spoke to teens about the Holocaust. "I remember that a girl in the back of the room got up and asked, 'What do you say to people who say it didn't happen?' "

The room became deathly silent.

"Then Mom looked directly at the girl and said, 'I wish they were right. When a doctor requests a complete medical history from me, I have to explain that I don't have one. My mother was killed when I was eight, and all the female relatives in my family were murdered in the Holocaust.'"

The doctor jots down her words and never asks again.

• • •

Robbyn, a published author, was a teenager when her father married Paula in 1981. (She calls Paula Mom, and Paula refers to Robbyn as her daughter.) "At that time, Mom never said anything about the Holocaust," she says.

"She didn't talk about it at all. She spoke about where she was born in a very general way. Novogrudek never came up. She never mentioned Belarus or the forest.

"I was about 14 when we went to San Diego on a trip. We were watching a movie about World War II. Mom casually said that she had seen people next to her getting shot. And that was it. She didn't elaborate.

"As I got older and learned about the Holocaust, I realized that she was caught in that hell. She came to the U.S. in 1949. Her mother was dead. Paula didn't have any of her mother's belongings, not even a photograph."

Robbyn, whose partner Jade is a physician, spent hours recording Paula's journey in the Holocaust. She feels she understands Paula's perceptual field.

"When you're a teenager, life seems very dramatic," she laughs. "But Paula was always telling me, 'Things are not so dramatic as you think.' In other words, they can be a lot worse.

"Paula was a child, faced with nameless, inchoate horrors. It might have been different if she had been older. She could have put a name to it. But how do you wrap your mind around something like that when you're seven, eight or nine?"

In those early days in Chicago, survivors vacillated between the impossibility of forgetting and the psychological necessity of integrating the past into their normal waking lives.

"Everyone just wanted to get on with it," Robbyn says. "You smile. You put on your lipstick, your best clothes. Did you know Paula was an incredible dresser when she was younger? That required a lot of energy. It must have been exhausting.

"But what else are you going to do? You're going to go forward, because there is no other direction. I think it takes quite a bit to be Paula — to put that behind you, for as long as you can, and get on with it."

Third-Generation Seeds

Jessica, 32, is the eldest of Paula's nine grandchildren. For her college entrance exam, she did not brag about personal accomplishments or elucidate her academic goals. Instead Jessica described something that happened when she was only 13. She wrote about secrets, a common thread uniting third-generation survivors.

"It had to do with my grandmother," she says. "I was a kid. I knew *Bubbie* was in the Holocaust, not in the camps but in a forest, because she had just started speaking to school-children about her Holocaust years. But she never spoke about this to us — and it was understood that we didn't bring up the Holocaust to her.

"Then one morning out of the blue, when I was in the eighth grade, I saw my grandmother on the front page of Denver's major daily newspaper. I didn't have time to read it, but as soon as I got to school I skipped my first period class and went straight to the library for a copy."

Jessica read the article, which covered Paula's talk at a middle school. "One of the first things she said was, 'When

I'm done today, you'll know more about me than my own children and grandchildren.' And I just lost it. I sobbed. I couldn't stop crying. I couldn't understand why she told children my age a story that she never shared with her own granddaughter."

Not long after that, Jessica attended a public event and listened to Paula speak about the Holocaust. After she finished, members of the audience were invited to contribute their own comments. "I got up on stage and I started to cry," Jessica remembers. "I couldn't say anything at all. I realized the connection I had to the Holocaust, and how these terrible things were a part of *my* life."

Jessica never met her great-grandfather Wolf, but she feels his actions were a testament to human willpower over circumstance and having trust in the outcome. "It takes a pretty impressive person to be as resourceful as he was. Also, a man who is that successful rescuing his kids, finding them food and a community, has to have a little luck.

"Maybe my great-grandfather Wolf was a shining star in a dark cloud."

Jessica is concerned that the Holocaust is being relegated to a dry historical fact. "It lacks a visceral bond. As the generations of survivors pass away, you begin to lose the personal connection.

"I feel like I am a survivor of the Holocaust, but not like the survivors themselves," Jessica says. "If the Holocaust was intended to eradicate the Jewish people — yet here we are — then that's an indelible part of who I am."

Her grandmother's generosity of spirit is a source of awe and humor. "I'll come over and say, '*Bubbie*, I like your shirt.' I'm just paying her an honest compliment. And she says, 'Take it! I want you to have it.' She's always asking whether I'm hungry, or if she can feed me a little something. There's nothing she wouldn't give you."

• • •

Alex, 22, surmises that he knew his grandmother was a Holocaust survivor since he was four years old, "as soon as I could comprehend the idea. It wasn't a secret. It was never taboo.

"My father's mother doesn't like to talk about the Holocaust. She was in the camps. But Grandma has been really open about it. She's never held anything back. She spoke at my elementary school, middle school, high school, even my college."

Being a third-generation Holocaust survivor "impacts my identity because of what my grandparents and relatives had to go through to get to where they are today," Alex says. "I can never forget what it means to be a Jew.

"Jewish kids my age will not let the memory of the Holocaust fall away, especially since history tends to repeat itself. If my generation forgets, then what would prevent it from happening again?"

Non-Jewish students' relationship to the Holocaust is another matter, he stresses. "I'm not saying that if you aren't Jewish you are ignorant of the Holocaust. But you might not be impacted in the same way as a second- or third-generation survivor.

"It's like if you asked me about slavery. Slavery existed in America. It's a fact, it was terrible, and I can never get that out of my mind.

"But I'm not African American. My direct relationship is with people who were in the Holocaust. To non-Jews, the Holocaust might well be more of a footnote. This applies to anything you study.

"If it's not relevant to your own experience, you will see it from a purely academic perspective," he says. "It's a skewed view, and a very hard question."

Alex says he will personally keep the memory of the Holocaust alive "through my heritage, my children, and informing them of my grandparents' history. I hate thinking about it, but it's a sad, unavoidable fact that my grandparents won't always be here. If people stop telling the story — if I stop telling the story — it will just disappear."

His grandmother doesn't want anyone to experience hatred: not the Jews, Muslims, Christians, or even the little boy being bullied in school.

"She is the most compassionate woman I've ever met in my life," Alex says. "She'll always tell you you're right, even if she thinks you're wrong. She is amazing. I love her."

• • •

Sarah, 21, possesses a penetrating intelligence that exceeds her years. "She's an old soul," Paula says often.

"I have known my grandmother was a Holocaust survivor since I can remember," Sarah says. "I don't think it was because she talked about it, at least when I was younger. At first it was like, 'This is something our family experienced.'"

Sarah has occasionally observed lingering trauma in her grandmother. "It's true that she's very forward moving. But if something isn't going well or isn't exactly perfect, she kind of retreats. Then she moves on."

As a third-generation survivor, Sarah feels "an ethical responsibility — and also that I have a particular opportunity.

"The Holocaust certainly was not the only time that people have been persecuted for who they are. Genocide is not over. It's happening right now." Sarah has started a non-profit group that works with refugees in the U.S.

She is aware that when Paula first arrived in America, survivors intentionally refrained from discussing the Holocaust. "There was a stigma attached to being a survivor. It was not a welcome subject. You didn't dwell on where you came from.

"That disconnect is interesting in terms of how the Holocaust continues to be a selectively told story in our family. It's as though there's a right time to talk about it, and a time to avoid it."

Unless she feels it's relevant to a particular situation, Sarah doesn't generally tell people that she's a third-generation Holocaust survivor. "Every family has their secrets. I don't walk up to people and say, 'Hi, I'm a third-generation Holocaust survivor.' That would be rather off-putting, don't you think?

"Even though it has influenced what I choose to do, I don't necessarily use it to define my identity. The Holocaust is a selectively told story in terms of who *I* am."

While a plethora of archival information on the Holocaust exists due to abundant Nazi documentation, survivors did not take photographs in the camps or the forests. "There are no pictures of my grandmother from that time," Sarah says. "There are no videos, no DVDs. So how do you make use of the record that is available, and acknowledge the record that isn't?"

Sarah recently watched "A Film Unfinished," a documentary that combines footage from a 1942 Nazi propaganda film about the Warsaw Ghetto with a newly discovered reel depicting the gruesome reality behind the staged fantasy.

"I knew my grandparents were never in the Warsaw Ghetto, but I found myself looking for their faces as I watched the film," she says. "I wanted proof, even though I *knew* they were in the Holocaust. There's something about the lack of tangible memory."

Yet Sarah finds it difficult to press Paula for her Holocaust memories. "I want so many details, but I'm very aware of the pain this would cause her. Remembering is its own animal."

During Rosh Hashanah and Yom Kippur, Sarah is overcome by the powerful significance of her grandmother's ordeal as a child. "I always think that my freedom to attend synagogue is due to both my grandparents," she says.

"But it feels inauthentic for me to say that they fought for my right to pray as a Jew, because I don't think that was their intention. They fought to stay *alive* — and there's nothing wrong with that."

'I Have to Tell the Story. That's Why I Survived'

I slowly climb the stairs to Ponderosa High School in Parker. My ankle tells me it's going to snow, if not tomorrow then the next day. Despite the fact that I've spoken to students about the Holocaust for 17 years, I still feel a little surge of stage fright each time.

Dr. Mark Thorsen, the teacher, waits for me behind the front doors and welcomes me with a hug. A 2010 U.S. Holocaust Memorial Museum fellow, Mark is dedicated to rescuing the Holocaust from academic and historical neglect.

This is my third visit to Ponderosa, located 25 miles outside of Denver amid rolling hills and suburban strip malls. Following my talk, I will invite the 11th-grade class to paint with me.

Although I don't follow a script, I do utilize a plan that enables me to interact with students on a positive level. First I share this horrible story. But I refuse to leave them with an image of a wounded animal. I play with them in a humorous way so they can see me as normal person.

Some Holocaust speakers begin their narratives in hell and conclude in hell. I'm not making judgments. But this isn't what I choose to project. I want these innocent minds to meet a woman who triumphed over trauma and enjoys a full and rewarding life.

The guard checks my driver's license. A tall girl approaches Mark and delicately asks whether it's OK to eat a candy cane in the classroom. Unaware of my identity, she's apparently worried that enjoying this simple pleasure might offend the guest Holocaust survivor. "Of course it's OK," Mark says.

"I'm really nervous," adds a friend of the girl holding the candy cane. Her anxiety is understandable. To her, a Holocaust survivor is a grim-faced, wizened statistic. She will hear bitter truths in that room. She will also laugh, *with* me.

The desks are arranged in a semi-circle. Chicago sports pennants and signs flank the walls: Chicago Cubs Avenue; Reserved Parking, Bears Fans Only; Chicago Blackhawks. I learn this is Mark's homage to his past. He probably doesn't remember that I lived in Chicago after the war.

I sit in front of the blackboard and introduce myself. "Hi, I'm Paula Burger." The students smile hesitantly, their 16-

year-old faces opening like pink buds. They are ready to absorb me.

During my 20-minute talk I include details I would never mention to fifth graders. These students, however, are old enough. Then I encourage questions. This is the heart of what I do, and why I do it. A reticence I fully anticipate hangs in the air. Where younger kids rush in, older students often refrain.

Finally a male student in the back raises his voice.

"How did you stay warm in the winter?"

"We did not stay warm in the winter," I say matter-of-factly.

The ball is in motion. A girl wants to know what happened to the doll I brought to the ghetto. I hear that one a lot. Students frequently utilize memories from their own childhood to enter mine.

Questions both practical and profound accelerate around the room. "Why did you come to Colorado?" "Like everyone else. I visited!" I add that my grandson is graduating Colorado State University this weekend. "And boy, was it a long haul!" They laugh because this is their future, too.

I let the students know that I empathize with universal teenage conflicts. It pulls them closer. I tell them about the time I told my children that we were moving to Colorado. "And of course they did as they were told," I say sarcastically. "Don't you always do what your parents tell you to do?" "Oh yeah, right," they commiserate. "I thought so," I grin.

Serious questions are treated seriously. And they are abundant.

"What was daily life like in the ghetto?"

"Children disappeared. Killing was routine. It wasn't something you accepted, but eventually you adopted a kind of stoicism."

"Does your brother tell his story to people?"

"Isaac was born in 1939. He was so young when the war started. He remembers holding my hand and walking through a green field. He doesn't remember our mother at all. That's very sad. But he also didn't feel that much pain when she was gone. So . . ."

"How did you keep going in the forest?" a girl frames her words carefully.

"It was cold. People chased you, tried to kill you."

"Why didn't you give up?" She is perceptive, sensitive.

"I think the human spirit wants to survive. You go day by day, hoping the next morning will be better. Then you wake up and it isn't, but you still hope the next one will be better. We never thought we'd survive. We had no reason to believe that. But you still go on.

"I don't have a good explanation. You just go on. It's like having a terminal illness. You live one day at a time even though you know you're going to die."

"Have you ever returned to your hometown in Poland?"

"No," I answer emphatically. "When my husband and I went on a trip to Russia and Poland in 1999, our group was about 30 kilometers from my hometown. If I knew where my mother was buried, I would have visited her grave.

"But my home? I come from a place where everybody tried to kill me for no reason. My only crime was being Jewish. I will never go back there."

"Are you still Jewish?"

"Yes. Are you surprised?"

The dark-haired questioner squirms slightly. "Well, I just didn't know if it was still something you wanted to be."

"This is an excellent question," I begin. "Some Jews who survived the Holocaust did reject their faith. They felt, 'I've had enough, I'm not interested, I don't want my children to go through this nightmare.' But the truth is, religion is not something you pick. You're usually born into it.

"My parents were Jewish. My grandparents were Jewish. My great-grandparents were Jewish. It's the only religion I know. I celebrate our holidays, not because I think they're better than yours, but because they are mine."

A diminutive girl wearing large glasses and a knitted cap asks a pointed question: "Have you ever struggled with survivor's guilt because you lived and millions died?"

I could equivocate, or lie.

I do neither.

"No. I am very happy that I survived. I'm sorry that six million Jews died, but I don't feel responsible. I've never related to survivor's guilt. I am here today to tell you the story. That's why I survived. Otherwise, there is no reason."

I survey the room and notice sixth-period yawns here and there. I stand up. "OK," I challenge them. "Who wants to paint?" Suddenly they are timid again. "Listen, if you don't want to do this, you don't have to," I say.

Suddenly they rush to the table Mark has covered with white canvas, brushes and five palettes of yellow, white, red, blue and green paint.

"What do you want to paint?"

Silence.

I explain that landscapes and flowers are the easiest subjects. "You can be very creative. And you don't need to know how many petals a rose has or the number of leaves on a tree."

Mark projects a lovely landscape on a wide screen behind the table. I feel the students' distaste.

"OK, the holidays are coming up," I suggest. "Let's paint a Christmas tree." These kids have no idea I am well known for my Chanukah menorahs. Much like a doll or a pet can help a child open a window on the Holocaust, I sense that painting Christmas trees might be these teenagers' portal into art.

Tentative hands reach for brushes and gravitate toward the blue paint.

"Start with the sky," one girl recommends to her friends.

Their small brushes limit broad, impressionistic strokes. I grab a larger one, make a deft, swirling motion and a cloud materializes. The group is amazed. And I'm delighted.

"Kids, I have to go!" I announce. "I have a hair appointment in an hour!" Some students concentrate too hard on a line or curve to look up. Those who hear me laugh and wish me well.

I stop for a second at the classroom door. These 16-year-old students braved the horror of my childhood and survived. I want their last image of me to be an energetic woman dashing from the Holocaust to a beauty shop.

Outside the school, I bundle up and walk down the steps to my car. I notice the pain in my ankle has disappeared. Scanning the clouds, I wonder: "Papa, did you see these kids? Can you see me at all?"

Epilogue

A late December wind rearranges patches of snow in Denver's Mt. Nebo Cemetery, where my father is buried. His headstone is deceptively simple. It does not say "Holocaust survivor" or suggest anything heroic.

The only thing that separates Wolf Koladicki's modest monument from the others is a missing birth date lost in the insanity of war.

Several rocks of various shapes and sizes line the top of the headstone. According to tradition, Jews leave rocks to indicate that love has paused here. I lift my head toward the Rocky Mountains. I see the Naliboki.

I was a little Jewish girl in the most heinous decade of the 20th century. For more than two years I have told and retold my story for this book. I feel as if I've aged 10 years.

It was terrifying enough to be a child in the Holocaust. Why go back again and again?

I have made numerous choices in my life. Being a witness is not a choice. It is a sacred responsibility. I tell my story to honor the six million that didn't make it.

My mother Sarah is one of them, her beauty and grace severed in the prime of life. I spent eight precious years in her arms — and decades aching for them.

The children I played with in the ghetto belong to that vast silence. The Nazis murdered six million of us and left not a single headstone. My words hallow anonymous ground.

Two funeral processions have passed through the cemetery gates since I arrived. We all die. If you don't believe me, just look around you.

After Mama was killed, I wanted to give up. When Papa disappeared for weeks in the forest, I willed myself to die. I guess death didn't want me.

Like the snowflakes of my childhood, we swirl, struggle, collapse — but as long as we breathe, we are commanded to live.

I see shadows of myself in the students I meet, especially the younger ones. Kids from one-parent homes often feel abandoned. Their heads hang so low. Others are bullied day after day for no apparent reason.

I tell these children they can survive anything. Just look at me. The Holocaust could have rendered me an eternal victim.

I rejected the part and devoted myself to the menorah's light.

The pleasure I derive from my family transcends margins on the page. Despite time's passage, Isaac is still my sweet brother. Sam is the love of my life. As I watch my children and grandchildren embrace life's journey, the storm that once raged inside me has subsided.

It is my hope that I can help people become more compassionate and reach out to those suffering pain and loss. Acting humanely is not a given. It too is a choice.

Papa, it's time for me to go home. Sam is waiting.

I'm putting a beige stone on your headstone. You loved the color beige. I never knew why. You saved us from the hungry jaws of hell. Without you there would be no children or grandchildren to kiss, no husband waiting for me, no story to tell.

Sleep well my dark star. You are the reason I feel this winter sunlight on my face.

I love you,

Paula

Afterword

Paula Burger has an astonishing memory for events that took place under extreme duress 70 years ago. Just seven when the Nazis occupied her hometown of Novogrudek, Poland, in 1941, she was 10 when the Russians liberated the Bielski partisans in 1944. She was a child.

Paula and I sat together every Sunday morning at her kitchen table. The seasons came and went, much like they did in the Naliboki — the chill of autumn, rain, snow, the first flowers of spring, green summer grass, the return of fall.

As I took notes on the laptop and recorded her memories, she often stopped and glanced through the window. I did not disturb her reverie.

Normally Paula is a very upbeat and funny lady. Ask anyone. But repeatedly returning to the Holocaust drained her energy. She would pick at the breakfasts she made for us or idly draw red flowers on white napkins.

I never told her this, but often at the end of a session I ran inside the elevator down the hall, waited until the doors closed and cried. This project was difficult for both of us.

There were no calendars in the Naliboki. If Paula was unable to supply a specific date, I consulted *Defiance: The Bielski Partisans* by Nechama Tec (1993) and Peter Duffy's *The Bielski Brothers* (2003) to give the reader a chronological context.

I am indebted to Paula Burger for sharing her story with me. I hope that this book pays tribute to her courageous will and tenacious spirit. She has touched me profoundly.

It's impossible to change the past, but the future is a choice.

I pray we choose well.

Andrea Jacobs,

Denver, Colorado

Biographies

Paula Burger was born in 1934 in Novogrudek, Poland. She survived the Holocaust with the Bielski partisans in WW II and immigrated to America in 1949. Burger, who discovered painting at age 12, studied under artist Mort Schneider and later attended the Art Students League of Denver. Her landscapes, abstracts and signature menorahs are in private, public and corporate collections throughout the world. Paula regularly talks about her Holocaust experiences to students at Denver-area schools and for other organizations. Married to Sam Burger, she has four children and nine grandchildren.

Co-author Andrea Jacobs, a St. Louis native, is the senior writer at the **Intermountain Jewish News** in Denver. Jacobs has won multiple first-place awards in feature writing, personality profiles, arts and criticism, news and investigative journalism from the Colorado Press Association and the American Jewish Press Association. A journalist for 27 years, she earned a B.A. in English literature from Drake University.

Paula and Isaac

Paula and Isaac at the tribute dinner honoring Commander Tuvia Bielski and his brothers and celebrating the partisans of the Bielski Brigade, New York City, Oct. 28, 2013.

Photo by: Keren Traub